Scrapbooking with Photoshop® Elements

The Creative Cropping Cookbook

Lynette Kent

SYBEX® San Francisco • London

Publisher: DAN BRODNITZ
Acquisitions Editor: BONNIE BILLS
Developmental Editor: MARIANN BARSOLO
Production Editor: ERICA YEE
Technical Editors: HOWARD GOLDSTEIN, TANDIKA STAR
Copyeditor: KIM WIMPSETT
Compositor: FRANZ BAUMHACKL
Graphic Illustrator: KATE KAMINSKI
Proofreaders: JAMES BROOK, NANCY RIDDIOUGH
Indexer: TED LAUX
Book Designer: FRANZ BAUMHACKL
Cover Designer: CARYL GORSKA
Cover Illustrator/Photographers: CARYL GORSKA, LYNETTE KENT

Library of Congress Card Number: 2004109317

ISBN: 0-7821-4377-6

Manufactured in the United States of America

10 9 8 7 6 5 4 3 2 1

To my children, who are the greatest even though they think

their mom is weird to get excited about technology.

And to my fantastic parents, who just know.

 # Acknowledgments

I always thought authors wrote books. In reality it takes a talented and devoted team. Everyone at Sybex has contributed to this book. Dan Brodnitz offered encouragement; Erica Yee skillfully devised a publishing schedule that worked; Rodney Koeneke followed the coupon trail; the technical editors, Howard Goldstein and Tandika Star, made the work accurate; Franz Baumhackl and Kim Wimpsett made the pieces fit; and Kate Kaminski turned my rough sketches into works of art. Thanks to Bonnie Bills for going out on a limb to embrace a new concept. And most of all, a really big thank you to my virtual coauthor Mariann Barsolo, who organized my writing and my thought processes.

Many thanks to all the people at various companies who spent hours answering my technical questions on hardware: my friend Anna Jen of Maxtor; Peggy Daniel of Nikon; Mark Mehall, Bill Lindsay, and Jim McCartney of Wacom; Scott Heath and John Lamb of Canon; Sandy Gramley and Frank Fellows of HP; Ann Johnson of Porter Novelli for HP; Reed Hecht, Andreas Goehring, Monica Morita, Fabia Ochoa, Farideh Sherbaf, John Quinones, and Jack Duchinsky of Epson; Mary Ann Whitlock and Michael Ford of Microtek; Sergio Vera and Melody Chalaban of Belkin; Mickey Lass and Tom Kelley of PhotoWorks; Bob Howes of Lineco; Drew Hendrix of Red River Papers; Gregory Schern of Moab Papers; Stephanie Robey of PhotoSpin; Liz Quinlisk, Sandra Sumski, and Paul Hultgren of GretagMacbeth; Dave Klenske of Lexar; Mike Wong of SanDisk; Brian Twede of Claudia's ClipArt; and Mark Seastrand of *Creating Keepsakes*. Special thanks to Robin Williams for her personal encouragement, for her friendship, and for her many books that consolidate what I learned long ago in art school.

I'd also like to thank Chris and Rosario Cooper for conveniently getting married just when I needed to take photographs, as well as my friends Joyce, Amber, Matthew, Amy, and Olivia Cooper for allowing me to use photos of them for this book, and thanks to Nancy Gabriel for the wonderful shots of Matt. Thank you to Leigh Redfern for the great red-eye snapshot and to Michael Salas for the photograph of Nathalie.

Many thanks to Jean-Marc and Nathalie Corredor, and Lee, Monette, Rick, Beth, Eric, and Colette Kent who not only allowed me to work with photos of them but gave me some of their photographic work for the book as well.

And the biggest thank you to Rick Redfern, the most knowledgeable pixel prestidigitator of them all, for always being available to answer technical Photoshop, photography, and pixel questions at every resolution.

Foreword

I'm so excited to get my hands on this book! As founding editor of *Simple Scrapbooks* magazine, I'm fully aware of the excitement surrounding digital photography and what scrappers call computer-generated scrapbooks. I know that "digital" is here to stay and that it's going to change for the better the way I organize and share my photos and celebrate and preserve my memories. But I have to be honest, I still don't get it. I mean, exactly where are my pictures? Do I need a new scanner? How do I create these cool effects that I see? Let's say I create a virtual layout—then what? I try and share this lack of confidence with my tech-savvy friends and they say, "Oh come on, it's easy, just pick up some photo-editing software and start playing." Easy, I say … easy for you. I'm not a dummy, so how come I feel like one?

Thank heavens for Lynette Kent. Lynette is a sought-after trainer with years of professional experience helping people learn new technologies. Lynette knows digital and what she wants most is to remove the "techie intimidation" factor and guide people like me successfully through the maze of information, techniques, and acronyms surrounding the use of cameras, scanners, printers, monitors, and other equipment. I first met Lynette a couple of years ago at a scrapbooking event, where I had to squelch the urge to invite her to my house for a weekend of one-on-one. I knew after a few moments of encouraging conversation that there was hope for me. She didn't talk down or act as if I should know more than I do. She just listened and answered my questions. Now, with her book, my dream of a one-on-one is a reality. I can literally take Lynette and her knowledge and experience home with me.

I love that instead of offering a myriad of software options, Lynette is centering her teaching on Photoshop Elements. Photoshop Elements is the number one consumer photo-editing software. It's got everything I need, from tools that enhance my photos to intuitive options for categorizing and finding them—and Lynette brings it all to life. You'll rejoice with me in page after page of step-by-step instruction and special features. I love the highlighted tips and notes and the fun recipe cards that I can pull out and take with me. Suffice it to say, my days of feeling like a "digital dummy" are numbered—what a relief!

Stacy Julian
Founding Editor
Simple Scrapbooks magazine

About the Author

Lynette studied art and French at Stanford University. After completing her master's degree, she taught at both the high-school and community-college level. She first used a computer to draw a company logo in 1988, since working with traditional art materials at home was difficult with children around. From then on, she was hooked on technology!

She has taken numerous technical training courses on software, hardware, and digital photography, and she has studied with early-adopter digital and photography gurus including Rick Redfern, Rick Valasek, Richard Chang, and Scott Kelby.

When Photoshop Elements was initially released, Lynette found it offered the perfect combination of photography and design tools for scrapbooking. She taught digital scrapbooking techniques to the editors of *Creating Keepsakes* magazine early on and has taught classes at various scrapbooking and other art venues. For the past 12 years, she has stayed ahead of the ever-changing technology curve by leading the Adobe Technology Exchange, an organization for professional graphic designers and photographers.

She still draws and paints with traditional media but enjoys finding digital ways to enhance any type of art project, especially scrapbook pages.

Contact the author at Lynette@kentdesign.org.

Contents

Introduction   *ix*

Chapter 1   **Page Rules**   **1**

The Rule of Balance 2
The Rule of Visual Center 3
The Rule of Thirds 5
The Rule of Negative Space 6

Chapter 2   **The Elements of Design Simplified**   **9**

Line 10
Shape 10
Mass 10
Texture 11
Value 12
Color 13
Type 15

Chapter 3   **Basic Principles of Design Really Simplified**   **19**

Proximity 20
Alignment 21
Repetition 24
Contrast 24

Chapter 4   **Take Your Best Shot! Digital Cameras**   **27**

Understanding Pixels 28
Types of Digital Cameras 28
Digital Camera Components You Should Know 29
The Care and Feeding of Your Digital Camera 37
Getting Your Photos onto Your Computer 38

Chapter 5   **Scanners Aren't Scary**   **41**

What to Look for in a Scanner 42

Creating Scanner-Computer Connections 45

Scanning Software 48

Planning Your Scan 49

The Care and Feeding of Your Scanner 52

Chapter 6   **Ink-Jet Printers: A Primer**   **55**

All Types of Printers 56

Choosing an Ink-Jet Printer for Scrapbooking 57

The Care and Feeding of Your Ink-Jet Printer 63

Printing with Photo Services 66

Chapter 7   **More Tools for Scrapbooking and Archiving**   **69**

Pen Tablet, the Mighty Unmouse 70

Monitors Matter 72

Preserving Your Images 74

Archiving Digital Files 76

Chapter 8   **Getting Started with Photoshop Elements**   **81**

Why Use Photoshop Elements? 82

Before You Start, Have a Backup 82

Organizing Your Files with Photoshop Elements 85

Photoshop Elements Editing Tools and Palettes 88

Chapter 9   **Photo Effects**   **95**

Quick Photo Fixes 96

Simple Photo Retouching in Standard Edit Mode 101

Cropping Techniques in Standard Edit Mode 106

Chapter 10   **Special Effects**   **113**

Frames and Mattes 114

Artistic Effects 117

Creative Effects 121

Chapter 11   **Text Effects**   **127**

Stylizing Editable Text 128

Adding Text to Photographs 130

Painting Text 131

Filling Text with a Background or Photo 134

Chapter 12   **Clip Art and Backgrounds**   **139**

Using Clip Art Collections 140

Creating Backgrounds 141

Scanning Backgrounds 144

Chapter 13   **The Full Page**   **149**

Scanning a Photograph, Slide, or Negative 150

Printing a Photo or Other Image 153

Building a Digital Page 154

Scanning a 12×12 Page with a Letter-Sized Scanner 160

Printing a Scrapbook Page 165

Appendix   **Easy Monitor Calibration with a Colorimeter**   **167**

Getting Your Monitor in Sync 167

Calibrating and Profiling 168

Index   *170*

Introduction

Photoshop Elements was designed for digital photography. In reality, Elements is the best and only software you need for digital scrapbooking. But to use the software, you need to have a computer and other obvious and not-so-obvious computer hardware and peripherals.

This book is a practical guide to understanding and using those peripherals for home photography, scrapbooking, and other crafts. Digital equipment such as digital cameras, scanners, and printers are some of the most powerful tools ever invented for communicating and preserving memories. But they often seem so complicated. This book demystifies all the technical terminology and numbers that surround digital equipment and guides you through purchasing decisions. It includes tech-support tricks for maintaining the hardware and shows you how to use digital equipment to make the most of your scrapbooking time. The projects included in the book are great starting points for digital scrapbooking. Remember, you aren't replacing scissors and glue, but rather you're adding new tools to your toolkit and new ways to archive your memories. Using a computer is still traditional scrapbooking—you just save time and money.

What You'll Learn from This Book

The first three chapters cover traditional design concepts and apply them to scrapbook pages. Use these for inspiration or to figure out why one of your pages looks better than another. **Chapter 1** illustrates simple page rules to help you design emotionally powerful pages. **Chapter 2** covers the elements of design as taught in many art schools but again applied to scrapbook page design. **Chapter 3** describes the principles of design and puts these in the context of scrapbooking design. Reading these chapters won't replace the years of study and experience of a professional graphic designer, but it will probably change the way you plan and look at scrapbook pages in the future.

Chapters 4, 5, and 6 offer simple technical explanations and tips for using digital cameras, scanners, and printers, respectively. **Chapter 7** shows how using graphic pen tablets makes working with a computer more creative and comfortable, and it explains what you should know about monitors. And since using a computer offers new ways to archive your photos, this chapter also includes information on other hardware peripherals with tips and techniques for digital archiving.

Chapter 8 introduces the interface and tools in Photoshop Elements 3. Chapter 9 focuses on improving photographs, and Chapter 10 covers adding more artistic and creative techniques to digital photos. The projects in Chapter 11 demonstrate ways to make your text and titles special, and Chapter 12 shows how to use clip art and background design elements. Finally, Chapter 13 illustrates how to scan a photo or a full 12×12 page, how to print page elements for use on a traditionally assembled page, and how to build a complete scrapbook page from scratch with Photoshop Elements.

In addition, the appendix shows you step-by-step how to calibrate your monitor with a colorimeter, so you can more accurately fix your photos. Then, in the very back of the book, you'll find coupons for purchasing some of the equipment discussed in Chapters 4–7, as well as tear-out recipe cards you can have handy to complete the most popular Elements projects in Chapters 8–13. Just look for the recipe card icon shown here for corresponding recipe cards.

Who Should Read This Book?

This book is not just for scrapbookers. The information is useful for anyone who has a computer and wants to improve his or her photos, albums, and craft projects. If you want to bypass the computer salesperson's geek-speak gibberish when you purchase basic equipment, or if you're lost in the maze of acronyms such as LCD, CRT, dpi, or ppi and just want to know how many pixels you *really* need, then this book is for you. If you are looking for creative guidelines for your scrapbook or album pages, read this book. If you want to scan photos easily or enhance digital photographs before you print, then use this book. And if you want to create parts of a scrapbook page or a complete page quickly, without any mess to clean up, then this book is definitely your starting point.

How to Use This Book

Like the subtitle implies, this is a cookbook. Use it! It includes *shopping lists* to take along to the store to purchase peripheral computer equipment, *coupons* with valuable discounts from a number of manufacturers, and *recipe cards* with abbreviated steps for many of the projects. You can even tear out the recipe cards and save them in a standard recipe card box.

Start by reading the table of contents. If you need ideas for a page design, check out the general design concepts to guide your own creativity. When you need to understand or want hardware products to add to your scrapbooking tools, go to the chapters that explain the hardware, copy the shopping lists, and check the coupons at the back of the book. If you already have digital files and Photoshop Elements 3 on your computer and want to fix photos or create page parts, start with Chapter 8 to get an overview of the Photoshop Elements interface and then go straight to the project you want to accomplish. Since it's difficult to memorize the steps in any project, keep the tear-out recipe cards next to your computer.

Note that this book doesn't cover every type of hardware available or every feature in Photoshop Elements. Instead it tries to simplify technical information and explains how to use the tools and software for scrapbooking and various craft projects. To explore more of the photography tools in Photoshop Elements, look for Mikkel Aaland's book *Photoshop Elements 3 Solutions* (Sybex, 2004). Mikkel explains Photoshop Elements from a photographer's perspective.

Platform Differences

Photoshop Elements is available for both Windows and Mac. However, the newest Photoshop Elements 3 adds one major feature called the *Organizer* for only the Windows platform. Macs already come with iPhoto, which has many of the same organizational tools. Other platform differences, such as those in the Photoshop Elements Browser, are easy to understand. The keyboard commands differ but only slightly. Throughout this book, we've included the Windows command first, followed by the Mac command. For example, when you see Ctrl+D / ⌘+D, you press the Ctrl+D keys in Windows or the ⌘+D keys on the Mac.

One Last Thought...

Since technology has already changed our lives, let's use it to preserve our memories.

Rosario
and
Christopher

May 29, 2004

Page Rules

Design is a visual language. With each scrap-book page, you tell a story. You want to guide your viewers' eyes to what you want them to see and feel. Everything you put on that page, where you place the items, and where you leave open areas, all help evoke the memory of an event. Furthermore, the design of one page can also direct the reader to the following pages, which may be a continuation of the story. In this chapter, you'll explore the four basic page rules. Use them as guidelines to help you create visually pleasing and emotionally powerful pages. Just remember, they all work together, and they work with the elements and principles of design, described in Chapter 2 and Chapter 3.

1

Chapter Contents

The Rule of Balance
The Rule of Visual Center
The Rule of Thirds
The Rule of Negative Space

The Rule of Balance

Balance is probably the most obvious rule of page design. The placement of the elements on a page affects the emotions of the viewer. A lopsided page, or one in which the elements and photos are placed in an unbalanced way, may make the viewer want to turn the page quickly.

Balance doesn't mean that everything is perfectly even. A balanced page may be divided in half, it may be divided in thirds, it may be divided into one third and two thirds, it may be divided into four even or uneven pieces. A balanced page may have one center of focus or several. The whole idea is that you can look at a balanced page for a long time and feel the story that it tells.

You can create balance in a page in many different ways. Balance can be *symmetrical*, where the design is centered or mirrored. Figure 1.1 shows some page designs that have symmetrical balance. Something is said to be *symmetrical* if you draw a centerline through it from top to bottom, dividing it in half, and it results in equal masses on both sides.

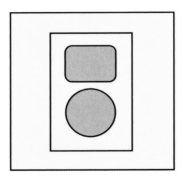
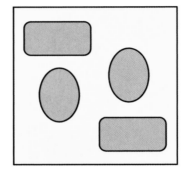

Figure 1.1
Symmetrical balance

Balance can also be *asymmetrical*, where the design is off-center; in other words, it includes uneven elements. Asymmetrical designs can lead the eye and create a sense of movement, as in Figure 1.2.

Figure 1.2
Asymmetrical balance

Balance may be *radial*, where the parts of the design actually radiate from a center or even swirl around the page, as in Figure 1.3.

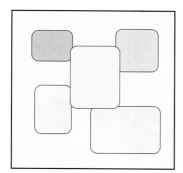

Figure 1.3
Radial balance

Radial balance can also exist without an object in the center of the page, as in Figure 1.4.

Figure 1.4
Radial balance without a
centered object

Do you see how the layout of the images in the sample scrapbook page in Figure 1.5 makes your eyes follow the story around the page clockwise?

Figure 1.5
Radial balance scrap-
book page

The Rule of Visual Center

The Rule of Visual Center is one often used by painters. This rule states that the most natural direction of eyes when looking at a page is to focus first on an area on the page or the canvas that's slightly to the right of and just above the actual center of the page, as in Figure 1.6.

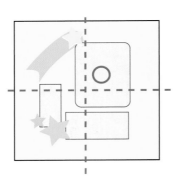

Figure 1.6
Visual center

Figure 1.7
Leonardo's *Mona Lisa*. Where do your eyes meet her eyes? The original is in the Louvre Museum in Paris.

In Leonardo da Vinci's *Mona Lisa*, people often say that her eyes follow the observer around the room. The reason is that Leonardo, a master from the Renaissance, used perspective to draw the way people see. In doing so he learned a number of tricks. He painted her pupils unevenly in her irises and then used the Rule of Visual Center. *Mona Lisa*'s eyes are looking at an area to the right and just above the center of the painting, and that's where viewers are looking. As viewers walk around, they're actually still staring at that same spot, so they think *Mona Lisa* is looking at them. Placing an item exactly in the center of a page makes a demand upon the viewers' eyes to stay at that point, resulting in a dull and uninteresting page. However, placing the most important information slightly off-center arouses interest and inclines the viewers' eyes toward continuous movement about the page (see Figure 1.7).

By placing the most important element or photo at this visual center, you're directing all the attention to this part of the page and saying, "Here's where the story begins." What's the first place your eye is drawn to on the scrapbook page shown in Figure 1.8? Notice how the diagonal red forms also lead you to the same spot.

Figure 1.8
On this wedding memory page, your eye is drawn just to the right and above the center of the page.

The Rule of Thirds

The Rule of Thirds is not only used by graphic designers but also by photographers. Remember this one when you take your photos as well as when you design a page. This rule states that designs are more interesting when the page is visually divided into thirds vertically, horizontally, or both and the most important elements are at the intersection of those thirds (see Figure 1.9).

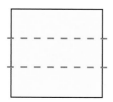 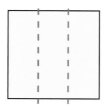 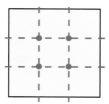

Figure 1.9   The Rule of Thirds

Photographers often use this rule by visually dividing their composition in both directions and centering the main object at one of the intersecting points. In Figure 1.10, notice where your eye lands, and look for the intersection of the thirds. See how the main subject, the Cathedral of Notre Dame, is centered at the top-right intersection? Notice also the direction of the Seine River as it curves up and around the cathedral? As the river narrows, it almost points to the cathedral in the upper-right third of the photo.

Figure 1.10
Even the bend in the river forces the eye to follow around to the right-top intersection of the thirds and toward the cathedral.

Using the Rule of Thirds, photographers often emphasize a beautiful sky or an expanse of land. The photo becomes more interesting by having the horizon line somewhere other than centered on the page. The evening sky in Figure 1.11 tells the story of a beautiful sunset.

Figure 1.11 The sky is the best part of this photograph, a view from Lahaina on Maui. The horizon line is in the center of the bottom third, allowing the two top thirds to show off the sunset and the mood.

Scrapbook pages often follow the Rule of Thirds either in one direction or in a combination. On the page in Figure 1.12, although you see only two photographs, the Rule of Thirds works well with the French flag as the background. The sketch of the Eiffel Tower balances the central section. Even without journaling, you know what happened on this trip.

Figure 1.12
In this scrapbook page, the blue, white, and red colors of the French flag are echoed in the thirds of this simple page, as are the three words— *Paris, France,* and *1998*—used to describe it.

The Rule of Negative Space

The Rule of Negative Space is so important to good design that it has two easy-to-remember nicknames: *Less Is More* and *White Space Is Your Friend*.

Negative space, also known as *white space*, is simply an area on your page that isn't filled with different elements. Negative space doesn't have to be white or black, but it should be free of distracting elements and should most often be only one color or value. Negative space helps the balance of the page and focuses the viewers' imaginations. Providing "less," or including fewer elements on the page, enables the viewer to experience "more" of the memory. Look at the two vacation scrapbook samples in Figure 1.13 and Figure 1.14. The first one is very busy with photos and many different type styles. The second page gives a calmer feeling. In the second vacation example, your eyes are drawn around the page, and you're able to focus on each photo and the journaling. Which page tells you more about the mood of the vacation?

Figure 1.13
Sunset on a wonderful
vacation with a busy feeling

Figure 1.14
Sunset on a wonderful vacation,
using the concept of "less is more"

One Last Thought…

Rules are often broken. Designers sometimes break the rules to achieve special effects or to emphasize something. Once you know the rules, you too can break them with purpose and design great scrapbook pages.

CLOWNING AROUND FOR THE CAMERA

1981

APRIL

The Elements of Design Simplified

Every item you put on a page—from photos to fibers—and how you put them together contribute to the mood of your scrapbook page. You're illustrating your memories, and the page design transmits the emotion of your message.

The elements of design are the building blocks of your page. Each photograph, fiber, journaling, or confetti is considered a design element. A photograph is a shape, journaling is an example of type, and confetti shows color. As you read, think of what types of items you can put on your pages that relate to each element of design.

2

Chapter Contents
Line
Shape
Mass
Texture
Value
Color
Type

Line

A *line* is a mark that connects two points. On a scrapbook page, you can draw lines, or they may be in the background paper or in the fiber you use. What makes each line different or gives it character is the way it goes from one point to the other. It can be straight or curved, long or short, solid, dotted, dashed, thin or thick, or even thin becoming thick. Lines help connect or separate areas on a page and can direct the viewer to the important areas.

Several lines together can form a pattern, suggesting texture or even movement. And even the simplest lines can convey different emotions. What do you think of when you look at evenly spaced vertical lines in a window? Is Zorro's mark the same dull *Z* you see in a novel? See Figure 2.1.

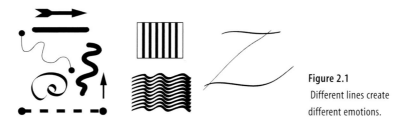

Figure 2.1
Different lines create different emotions.

Shape

A *shape* is a geometric or a natural form. Squares, rectangles, circles, ovals, and triangles are all geometric shapes. Leaves and snowflakes are examples of natural shapes. Even text is essentially a shape. Each letter and each character is an individual shape. And an area filled with journaling is a completely separate shape in and of itself. Shapes organize the information on the page. They can reinforce a theme or alter the feeling of the page.

Round forms are often comforting and humanizing. They can soften or feminize an image. When you see hearts and balloons, for example, you probably think of love, children, and happiness. Sharp corners and rectangles often convey a sense of order and strength. Lightning bolts and other jagged lines are visual alarms and show excitement. Look at each of the shapes in Figure 2.2 separately. Does the scroll remind you of an announcement? Do the balloons say "party"?

Figure 2.2
Shapes shape the mood of the page.

Mass

Mass is also called *volume* in design. It refers not only to the physical size of an object but also to the visual weight that it puts on a particular area of the page. A mass can be a solid item or a grouping of individual elements that look like one solid form, such as the balloons or the text-filled *T* in Figure 2.2.

Every item on your page contains mass. The way the visual volume of each piece relates to the other volumes on the page, and to the page as a whole, helps create the feeling of the page.

Look at the two page toppers in Figure 2.3. Each has a different visual mass. Which of the following words first come to mind for each page?

Happy…Proud…Bold…Whimsical

Figure 2.3
Different mass =
different meanings

Now look at the two photo pages in Figure 2.4. Cover the left side, and then cover the right. Does the one on the right seem larger?

Figure 2.4
These photos are the
same physical size but
have different visual
masses.

Texture

Texture can be both tactile and visual. In other words, you can add real fibers to your page to show texture, and you can create texture by simulating those fibers. Planned or not, texture is a part of every design. The scrapbook paper may have a textured surface that the reader can touch. Just gluing a photograph to a page creates a form of texture. The photographs themselves include different visual textures, such as skin, clothes, grass, wood, carpet, or animal fur.

Type can have texture, both as a pattern in the typeface and from embossing or beveling the individual letters. A page of type has a texture of its own. Squint your eyes, and this paragraph will look like a gray, textured area. You can also create visual textures with combinations of lines and shapes. By drawing rectangles superimposed on each other, you can create the illusion of a brick wall. Figure 2.5 shows visual textures that were created with lines and patterns.

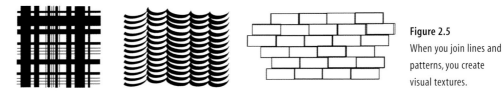

You can use both tactile and visual texture to reinforce a concept or to set the mood for the page. However, since texture is in every item, it's important to use it cautiously. Too many surface contrasts can compete for attention and confuse the reader. When the patterns and textures distract the eye from the intended message, it can overwhelm the main photographs. If type or journaling appears on top of a busy texture, the words could become unreadable. Again, the idea of the page is to communicate a memory, and you wouldn't want the message to be lost or confused in a mess of textures.

Value

Value is the lightness or darkness of an object, regardless of its color, or lack of it. Value, however, is determined only by the comparison of one object with one value to another object with another value. In other words, value is relative. Value also helps the page designer direct the focus of the page. Varying values on a page can show movement and lead the viewer's eye in one direction or the other.

Study the simple examples in Figure 2.6. Do you see the solid block areas first in the page on the left? Where is your eye drawn first in the middle example? Notice how varying the values in the box on the right lead you from the bottom up to the top of that sample.

Figure 2.6
Simples designs with differing values leave different impressions.

Value can be overpowered by one specific design element—color. We'll define color in the next section. However, look at the *grayscale*, or black-and-white, photograph in Figure 2.7. Where does your eye land first? Oh, the power of color!

Figure 2.7
The value is even here, but you're drawn to the color.

Color

Color refers to a point on the *visual spectrum*, or the range of light you can see with your unaided eye. Think of a rainbow. Sunlight goes through raindrops, which act as tiny prisms that break the light into colored wavelengths, ranging from violet through red. These are the colors the human eye can see. We think of color as red or blue, and the lack of color, also known as *achromatic color*, as white, gray, or black. Color has many aspects, and how you use colors in your page affects not only the colors themselves but also the mood you're trying to create.

Colored objects appear differently depending on the colors of the background or the colors of adjacent objects. A bright red car looks brighter set against a totally black background than on a street scene of mixed colors. Graphic designers often use a color wheel to determine what will work together. The color wheel starts with the *primary* colors of red, blue, and yellow. If you mix two primary colors, you get a *secondary color*. Specifically, you get purple from red and blue, green from blue and yellow, and orange from yellow and red. Carry that a step further, and you get *tertiary colors*, such as blue-green, mixed from blue and green, and so on.

The Color Wheel

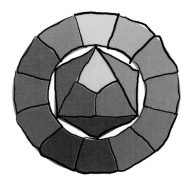

Colors that are next to each other on the color wheel harmonize with each other, and the effect is pleasing. Yellow and green are colors that are in *harmony*. Colors that are opposite each other on the color wheel are called *complementary colors*. Red and green are complementary colors, as are yellow and purple, or blue and orange. Complementary colors create extreme contrast and can create a visual vibration. A color that falls between two colors on the color wheel is called a *transitional color*. The amount of contrast created by two colors next to each other on a page depends on how many transitional colors are between the two on the color wheel. How much color harmony or color contrast you include on a scrapbook page depends on the message you're trying to communicate.

Hue, Lightness, and Saturation

In design terms, an actual color, such as pure red or pure blue, is referred to as *hue*. A hue can be warm or cool. Red, gold, yellow, orange, pink, brown, and burgundy are considered *warm hues*. They attract the eye and give the feelings of happiness, energy, or excitement. *Cool hues* usually include the areas on the color spectrum from green through violet, including all the blues and the shades of gray. Cool colors are considered more subdued and evoke feelings of freshness, purity, or tranquility.

Lightness refers to tints and shades of the pure color. A hue that's mixed with varying amounts of white creates a *tint*. Pink, for example, is a tint of red. Mixing different amounts of black with a hue creates a *shade*. Crimson, often called *dark red*, is red mixed with black. Therefore, crimson is a shade of red. Different tints and shades of the same hue offer many more color combinations and make different impressions on the viewer. Light colors such as pink, pale purple, and baby blue give the page a soft look. Dark brown, dark red, or dark blue may evoke a stronger, more regal theme.

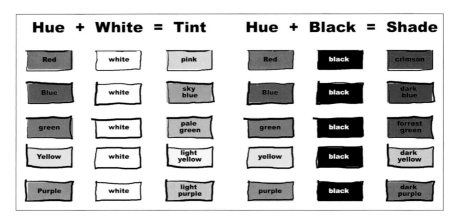

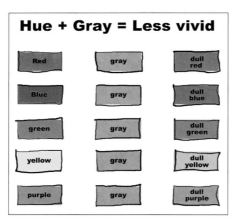

Saturation is the intensity of the color, or how vivid it appears. A vivid blue and a vivid red will have the same saturation, for example. You can create a dull red and a dull blue by adding gray to the pure hues. The saturation of the color gives it personality. Very saturated colors such as pure red and yellow hues shout at the viewer. Think of the vivid colors used in fast-food logos and menus. Dull, less-saturated hues speak softly and offer a blurry, more thoughtful feeling. Think of a blue-gray, misty, overcast sky on a beach. Pure white and black (although they're not colors but rather the absence or presence of light) are both vivid and make definite, strong statements.

Using Color Wisely

Color is the most dangerous element of design. It helps tell the story, sets the mood, and can push viewers away from or bring them into the page. Just as with excessive texture, too much or too strong a color can easily overwhelm and detract or distract from the intended message.

You must take into account the effect the colors you choose will have not only on your viewer but also on other colors on your pages. If you want your type to be legible, you want to choose colors that contrast enough with others but that don't bounce off the page. Colors that are too similar may just blend into one color blob.

The colors on the page include the colors in photographs as well as all the other images, words, and objects on your page. If the photo is bright and colorful, make the rest of your page softer but in harmony with those colors, so your central focus is prominent. If your photo has a soft feeling, make sure the background colors don't clash or overpower it. Too much color can ruin a page. Designers have a rather "colorful" way of describing the use of too much color. They call it "throwing up in color!" Take a look at Figure 2.8 and Figure 2.9. You don't need years of study in design to evaluate these two pages.

Figure 2.8
"Throwing up in color," or the use of too much color

Figure 2.9
In this example, the children become the focus of the page.

Type

Type not only verbally communicates the message of the page, but it's also a design element. Type can incorporate all the other elements of design. Each letter has a shape, and the shapes combine to make a larger shape. Each letter has a mass, and grouped together the text can form a volume of its own. The letters can have varied lines weights, thick or thin. The type can have texture, value, and color.

The words *typeface* and *font* actually have different meanings. A *typeface* refers to the specific design of the letters and characters regardless of size. A *font* is an assortment of letters and characters with the same features, in one style, such as italic or bold, and at one specific size. In traditional typesetting, a *font* was the collection of metal characters that were all the same style and one particular size. That distinction was important in the time B.C., or *before computers*. Today, although it may be technically inaccurate, you'll often see the two terms used interchangeably. Since fonts are now digitized, they can be changed to any size in the computer.

Why is a basic understanding of the different typefaces important? Each typeface expresses a different meaning and evokes a different set of responses in the reader, regardless of the words. The style, size, shape, and weight, and color all give a feeling before the viewer reads one word. And yet you want the text to be legible so that the viewer can read your words and feel the emotion of your page.

Although typographers distinguish many more categories, we will separate typefaces into only the following four groups: Serif, Sans serif, Script, Decorative.

Serif *Serif* typefaces, also known as *Roman* because they're derived from the letters chiseled into ancient obelisks and Roman arches, all have little tails on the letters. They can have varied thick and thin lines, or the individual lines can all have a similar weight. Look carefully, and you'll see that those tails or serifs create a continuous horizontal movement to the lines of type. This makes them easier to read for extensive text areas. Serif typefaces are used in most books, especially textbooks, as well as magazines and newspapers. Use serif typefaces when you're writing long journaling pages. When you use them as a headline, make sure they're big and bold.

Didot **Times** COPPERPLATE

Sans serif *Sans serif* typefaces, also known as *Gothic*, from the crude simplification of the Roman letters by the Gothic and other barbarians who conquered Rome, don't have those little serifs. *Sans* is the French word meaning "without"; hence, the letters in the sans serif fonts don't have serifs. Since sans serif typefaces have a clean and more technical look, they're often used in the illustrations and headlines in text and many educational books. Sans serif typefaces make good page toppers, or titles, for long journaling segments. They're also great when you're creating a special design or using type to crop your photos.

Arial Futura **Impact**

Script *Script* typefaces have a handwritten look. They seem to have been written with a pencil, a calligraphy pen, or even a brush. Use script typefaces carefully. Just like traditional handwriting, script can be hard to read when used for long blocks of text. Also, never use a script typeface in all caps. It's just unreadable. However, one large script capital letter at the beginning of a paragraph or sentence, or just by itself, calls attention to an area and can evoke beauty and elegance.

Chancery *Brush Script* *Edwardian Script*

Decorative *Decorative* typefaces are fun and different, but you wouldn't want to read an entire paragraph written in such a font. You could use a decorative typeface for the page topper or as an accent on a page.

ALMONT SNOW Curlz **Foo** WakeBake

Type Guidelines

In addition to understanding the types of type, you can follow certain guidelines to avoid visual headaches.

First, create strong contrasts between titles and paragraphs of text. Using contrasting typefaces helps bring out the meaning of the words. In the examples in Figure 2.1., the samples of text on the left use the same words as the ones on the right. Can you see how the stronger contrasts in the samples on the right make the point even more than the words themselves?

Second, graphic designers generally avoid using all capital letters, unless the typeface has only capital letters. All capital letters not only take up more space, but they're also less readable, as you can see in the example in Figure 2.11.

Figure 2.10 To contrast or not to contrast?

Figure 2.11 All capital letters can be difficult to read.

Finally, avoid creating a "ransom note" by using too many different typefaces on one page, as in Figure 2.12.

Figure 2.12
The "ransom note" style

One Last Thought...

Remember, everything that goes on the page is at least one element of design. Use the elements to build your page slowly. Plan the page with a minimal amount of items and fonts, and then step back and look at the page. If it tells the story, stop right there! You don't need to use every piece of clip art, every fiber, and every photo you have that fits your theme. Don't fill up the page. Fill your viewers' eyes with emotion instead.

50th
Wedding
Anniversary

Basic Principles of Design Really Simplified

In scrapbooking, just as in graphic design, you want the person looking at the page to understand the meaning of the event and to relive the moment. How can you make the viewer feel the pride of a graduation page or the adventure of a camping page? People won't read what's hard to read, and they won't look "into" a page that's confusing. The page always needs to be clearly planned and positioned. The most important part of the page must stand out, and the rest of the page should blend into the background.

In this chapter, we'll focus on the four most basic design principles and give you examples to help you apply them to your own scrapbook designs.

3

Chapter Contents

Proximity
Alignment
Repetition
Contrast

Proximity

Proximity is defined as being next to or very near. In design, the Principle of Proximity states that things that go together should be physically close to each other and grouped on the page. Items that are different or not as closely related should be separated. Using proximity on a page gives instant visual organization to everything on that page.

Let's consider a graduation page to illustrate how to use proximity. You have a photograph of the graduate. You may have a page topper, or you may create one with a decorative font and some special effects. You may also have some clip art showing graduation hats, a scroll representing a diploma, and some journaling. All these elements relate to the graduation photo. So where do you put these items on the page? The page in Figure 3.1 shows all these pieces. Notice how the spaces between the elements are almost equal, and no connections between the items seem to exist.

Figure 3.1
A graduation page with related but visually unconnected elements

Figure 3.2
A Graduation Scrapbook Page using the Principle of Proximity

Proximity doesn't mean you put everything in the same area on the page. The page elements that are in one visual group need to be connected to each other by their meanings. The viewer will then see grouped objects as one unit. Elements that aren't so closely related should be placed in separate areas. The Principle of Proximity brings visual organization to all the photographs and other page parts. If the message is clear, the page will be memorable.

In the case of the graduation page, you could put the graduate's photo near the page topper. You could place the journaling describing the event, the decorative clip art, and the mini-diploma in another group somewhere else on the page. Even though the page elements are all part of the theme, the headline and the photo really tell the main story. Any other photographs, clip art, or even the diploma are secondary. In Figure 3.2, you can see a possible layout for a graduation page using the Principle of Proximity. After you've read the rest of this chapter, look again at this sample. You'll also see the use of alignment, repetition, and contrast.

Alignment

The word *alignment* means to bring into a line and put in an order. The Principle of Alignment states that every item on a page should be connected to other parts of the page by an invisible line or multiple invisible lines. Even when the elements are separated from each other on different areas of the page, you should be able to see a visual connection from one item to the others and from each item to the page as a whole.

A page without alignment is chaotic, and all the objects in that page will appear to have been glued down wherever the page had room. The meaning of the page will be lost in the confusion.

To understand the alignment of different elements on a page, think of the arrangement of text on a page, such as the one you're reading right now. A block of text can be *left aligned*, or flush left, with each line of text starting on the same left vertical line. Text that's *right aligned* or flush right, has the end of each line of text forming a column on the right. When the middle of each line of text in a block falls along the same vertical line, that text is said to be *center aligned*. Look at the three sample text alignments in Figure 3.3.

Figure 3.3 Left-, right-, and center-aligned text

Groups of text don't have to be in the same area to be aligned to each other. They can be aligned and still exist on different parts of the page. In the example in Figure 3.4, the headline (or page topper) is aligned on the left with a block of text that's also left aligned. The headline is also right aligned with the flush right block of text near the bottom of the page.

Figure 3.4

Samples of different text alignments aligned to each other

The Principle of Alignment applies to all the elements on a page. A photograph can be aligned to another photograph or to clip art or journaling. And the elements can create vertical, horizontal or even diagonal visual lines anywhere on the page. Compare the samples in Figure 3.5 and Figure 3.6. The page in Figure 3.5 shows no common alignment between the elements. The page in Figure 3.6 shows the same elements using several types of alignment.

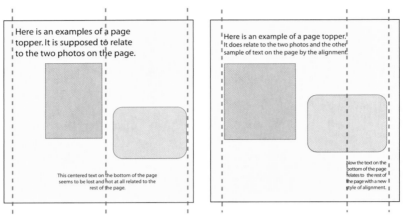

Figure 3.5 Mixed types of alignments without any visual connection

Figure 3.6 The left- and right-aligned text boxes visually relate to the image boxes, creating an organized look.

Try to find a strong visual line on your scrapbook page and stick with it. This visual line may be in a photograph or a combination of items. You can even combine items to create alignment. You may use right-aligned journaling on the left side of a photograph, as in Figure 3.7, arranging the right margin of the text with the line formed by the left borders of the photographs. In this case, the proximity of the two items helps group them even more. The journaling not only relates to the photos, but it's visually grouped with them by its alignment, as well as its proximity. Because we read type from left to right, each line of the paragraph leads us back to the image boxes and strengthens the connection between the meaning of the words and the content of the boxes. The viewer sees all the elements as one piece and immediately focuses on the message of the group as a whole unit. The two principles act in combination to create a visually organized page.

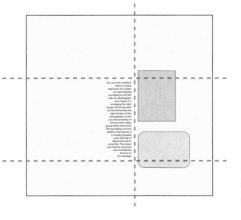

Figure 3.7
Alignment and proximity
working together

You can apply left, right, and center alignment to the elements in your scrapbook page layout. However, athough text can also be *fully justified* as it often is in newspaper articles and some books, avoid using this type of alignment for photos, clipart, and other elements on a scrapbook page. Fully justified means both the right and left sides of the text line up, forming a neat block. Fully justifying text may create an effective design element, but fully justifying all the objects on a page would mean evenly filling up or spreading out the individual parts. See how each item in Figure 3.8 is aligned with one edge and one corner?

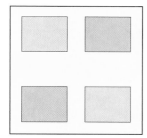 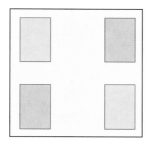

Figure 3.8
Block alignment using images isn't the best use of the space.

Such a design restricts eye movement on the page. It's organized, but it's also static and boring and would create an uneventful memory for a scrapbook layout. Look at Figure 3.9. It shows a page with all the elements in a fully justified alignment. Where's the focus of the page? Where's the emotion?

Figure 3.9
All elements with fully justified alignment

Figure 3.10
Changing the alignment of the page more accurately reflects the emotion of the event.

Changing the alignment, as in the example in Figure 3.10, changes the whole look of the page. By placing the photographs diagonally across from each other and tilting the main photo, the page catches the viewer's attention and tells a better story. This figure combines different alignments, increases the proximity of the parts, and adds the Principle of Contrast in one area for effect. The angled photo draws you right into the page to feel the emotion of the couple.

Repetition

By definition, *to repeat* is to say or do again what has already been said or done. The Principle of Repetition states that an item or items are repeated or used more than once on the page. Repetition in design is also known as *consistency*.

On a scrapbook page, you could use a piece of clip art several times, maybe varying the size each time. Another example of repetition would be using a specific shape for a photograph or a journaling box placed more than once on a page. Repeating a color on a page, as in a frame, in a border, or in a text box, is also an example of repetition.

Repetition, like alignment and proximity, visually organizes the information on a page to communicate a message. Think of business stationery. The logo, the colors, the type style, the alignments, and the shapes are repeated on the stationery and on the business card. Everyone who reads a letter or sees a business card will readily recognize the company.

Repeated elements in a scrapbook page not only add organization to the design, they also help unify the page to convey the message. The example is Figure 3.11 shows a page with almost no repetition. Although the theme of each item on the page is Valentine's Day, the overall look doesn't show unity or romance.

Now look at the sample page in Figure 3.12. How many repeated angles, curves, shapes, colors, and words can you find? Remember, any or all the elements of design may be repeated in various ways.

Figure 3.11
No repetition loses the meaning of the page.

Figure 3.12
Repeated elements unify this page.

Contrast

The Principle of Contrast is the easiest principle to understand and probably the most powerful when used properly. *Contrast* as a word means showing a noticeable difference when viewed as a comparison. To have contrast, you need more than one object. As a principle of design, contrast means that two or more items display completely different characteristics. And the key word here is *completely*. If the items are sort of different, but not enough so, they will actually confuse the viewer's eye rather than communicate the message.

Most often, a strong contrast involves more than just one characteristic. For example, an effective contrast between two objects may include both a large size difference as well as a difference in the shapes themselves. The most important thing to remember is that if two items in one area on a page aren't exactly alike, then make them really different.

In Figure 3.13, you can see two sample page layouts. Not enough contrast exists between the shapes on either page to create interest.

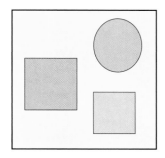
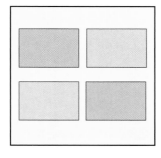

Figure 3.13
A lack of contrast loses the attention of the viewer.

Now look at the two sample layouts in Figure 3.14. These pages use shapes similar to those in the previous examples but are more interesting because of the contrasting sizes and placement. These two designs grab your attention.

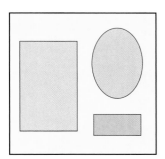
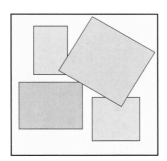

Figure 3.14
Pleasing design comes with contrast.

The purpose of contrast is to get something noticed. When you contrast two items, you're emphasizing one of them and creating an order of viewing. As with the other principles of design, contrast helps organize the piece to communicate your message more clearly. However, more than proximity, alignment, and repetition, contrast shouts at the viewer and says, "Here's the memory this page is saving."

One Last Thought...

The principles of design are interconnected. When you look at a well-designed page with strong alignment, you'll also see some form of proximity, repetition, and contrast. Study some finished pages that you find beautiful. Look where and how the design principles were used in each page layout. For your next cropping session, start with the principles, mix in your own imagination and creativity, and your pages will be the beautiful ones.

Take Your Best Shot! Digital Cameras

Today's digital cameras offer many more capabilities than traditional film cameras. Most professional photographers are going digital, and you'll be able to find numerous discussions as to the life and death of film cameras. For scrapbooking and crafts, a digital camera is one of the most useful tools you can add to your toolbox.

Whether you're in the market for your first digital camera or are just looking to understand the one you already have, you'll need to know the topics covered in this chapter. With so many models, you should understand what makes the camera click and what other items you'll need.

4

Chapter Contents
Understanding pixels
Types of digital cameras
Digital camera components you should know
The care and feeding of your digital camera
Getting your photos onto your computer

Understanding Pixels

Digital camera manufacturers are in a megapixel war. Advertising would have you believe that more megapixels means better photographs. That isn't necessarily true.

A *pixel* is a "picture element." It's the smallest unit of color or light in a digital image. A *megapixel* is one million pixels. The maximum number of pixels that a digital camera can capture relates to how big a print you can make from that photo and how sharp and detailed the image will be. However, just because one camera has more megapixels than another doesn't make it a better camera, and a larger number of pixels alone doesn't determine a better photograph. Other components inside the camera affect the quality of the pixels that capture the light, as well as the cost of the camera. Quality of pixels is as important as quantity, if not more so.

If you take photos with a film camera, your costs start going up as you buy and develop film. Since you can't see the shots when you take them, you may take several to be sure you get the right expression or lighting. And you pay for the developing even when the photos aren't any good.

With digital cameras, you can go crazy and take as many shots as your memory card can handle, copy them to your computer, clear the memory card and continue. Since you can see the images immediately when you take them, and since you can really study them on your computer screen, you'll print only the ones you want. Plus, reprints and enlargements later are more convenient with digital images and often less expensive than with film.

Types of Digital Cameras

Even at the consumer level, there are many digital camera models at varying prices. Most consumer *digital SLRs* (single lens reflex), cameras with separate and interchangeable lenses, and one piece compact digital cameras, including the digital "point-and-shoot" cameras, can produce photographs with better quality than their equivalent film cameras. However, still shots from a digital video camera generally do not have sufficient quality for scrapbooks. The best camera for your memories depends on how you take photos and on your budget. The Nikon D70 (Figure 4.1) and Canon Digital Rebel (Figure 4.2) are digital SLR cameras. The Nikon Coolpix (Figure 4.3) and the Canon PowerShot (Figure 4.4) are examples of compact, one-piece digital cameras.

Figure 4.1 Nikon D70 digital SLR camera. © Nikon Inc. All rights reserved.

Figure 4.2 Canon Digital Rebel SLR camera

Figure 4.3 Nikon Coolpix 3200. © Nikon Inc. All rights reserved.

Figure 4.4 Canon PowerShot S50

Digital Camera Components You Should Know

Digital cameras depend on a number of electronic parts to create the image.

Image Sensors

Photography is all about capturing light. In both film and digital cameras, a lens focuses light through an opening onto an area called the *focal plane*. Light is made of all the colors of the spectrum (red, orange, yellow, green, blue, indigo, and violet). In a film camera, a piece of film covers the focal plane. The colors from the light are transferred or translated onto the film when the light interacts with silver halide and other chemicals in the film. In a digital camera, an *image sensor* sits on the focal plane. The image sensor is an electronic chip composed of millions of microscopic elements. Each element corresponds to a pixel in the final image. These elements, called *photosites*, function as tiny buckets to collect the light during an exposure. The sensor may have two million pixels, as in a two-megapixel camera, or four million pixels, as in a four-megapixel camera, and so on.

Digital camera sensors are either CCD (charged coupled devices) or CMOS (complementary metal oxide semiconductor). Both have advantages; however, the explanations are beyond the focus of this chapter or this book. Both types of sensors are fine for scrapbooking photography.

The size of the image sensor in relation to the number of pixels on the sensor can affect the photograph. Image sensors can be as small as a fraction of an inch measured diagonally to almost two inches across. A very small sensor covered with two megapixels (or two million pixels) will have much smaller-sized pixels than a larger sensor covered with two million pixels. The larger the pixels, the more light the sensor can collect and the greater the variation in tones in the image. With a smaller sensor, the camera needs more pixels to produce a good tonal range or a good quality photograph.

AD Converter

Both CCD and CMOS sensors change the light into electrical signals. An *AD converter* (AD stands for *analog to digital*) converts the electrical signals to digital values. The digital information is then processed by an internal logic board in the camera that's basically a tiny computer. The quality of the AD converter is a major factor in the quality of your images.

Note: If the terms *analog* and *digital* seem confusing, think of a watch. A watch can be either analog or digital. In an analog watch, the face has an hour hand rotating around the face in a continuous motion. Digital watches have only numbers, or digits, on an LCD to tell you the time in precise numeric values. Since the natural world is analog, continuously moving in sequence, and computer tools work only with digits, digital cameras must convert what you see in order to process and record the analog information.

Lenses

Photographers often say that cameras are all about the glass. Lens quality is essential in both film and digital cameras. The better the quality of the optics, or the glass, the sharper the image and the better the colors in the photograph. A cheap, plastic lens will give you just that—cheap, plastic results. Since traditional camera manufacturers have been researching and improving the quality of their lenses for years, look for a brand that's also a traditional camera manufacturer when you shop for a digital camera. Nikon, Canon, Olympus, Minolta, Pentax, and Kodak are some of the best known. A digital camera with a quality glass lens may cost a bit more, but the quality of your memories depends on it.

Optical Zoom and Digital Zoom

Digital cameras often include two types of zoom: *optical zoom* and *digital zoom*. Some digital cameras are advertised showing the optical zoom multiplied by the digital zoom capabilities, as in "3× optical zoom plus 2× digital zoom equals 6× combined zoom." But that's misleading.

The only real zoom is the optical one. Optical zoom refers to a lens that can change the focal length from a wide angle to a telephoto. A wider angle provides a wider field of view. A telephoto lens narrows the field of view and the objects appear closer. (see Figure 4.5).

Figure 4.5 An example of a photo taken at the wide angle setting or no zoom (left) and one using optical zoom (right)

Comparing focal lengths between digital and film cameras may get confusing. The *focal length* of the lens, as in a 38mm lens, determines the area that will fit in your photo: the smaller the number, the wider the angle of view, and conversely, the larger the number, the narrower the view. Because the size of the sensor in a digital camera is generally smaller than the size of traditional 35mm film, the field of view on a digital camera will be narrower and objects will appear closer than on a film camera with the same size lens. For example, a 23mm lens on a digital camera may show an area equivalent to a 38mm lens on a film camera. The digital camera specifications often quote a traditional film camera equivalent for the lens plus the optical zoom. For example, a digital camera with a 23mm lens and 3× zoom would have the same range as a film camera with a 38–114mm zoom lens. And since each camera or brand can have a different size of sensor, the comparison is more complicated. Use the numbers only for reference. Try the camera in the store. Use no zoom to see how wide an area you can see. Then push the optical zoom button to its maximum and see how close far-away objects appear.

Digital zoom is nothing more than cropping the image, keeping the center portion and then magnifying the resulting image. This type of zoom doesn't increase the amount of detail visible in the picture. The camera focuses on the whole image, and the digital zoom cuts off everything but the center. The details are then digitally enlarged, producing a slightly "grainy" image. To get the image size back up to the size of your other photographs, the camera sometimes adds *interpolated* pixels to fill in the space. Interpolated pixels are "fill-ins," ones that the computer invents and adds by comparing and calculating the existing pixels in an image. So, using the digital zoom to take pictures may reduce the quality of the images you take, as in Figure 4.6.

Figure 4.6
Using digital zoom on top of optical zoom

Resolution and Compression

Digital cameras are most often described by the number of pixels on the sensor, or the maximum *resolution* of the camera. The greater the number of pixels, the larger the print you can make from an image. As a rule of thumb, a picture shot with a two-megapixel camera can be printed up to 5×7 inches, a three-megapixel camera can make prints up to 8×10 inches, and a good four-megapixel camera can make prints up to 11×14 inches.

Most digital cameras also include settings for image size (or resolution) and one for image quality (or compression). In other words, if you use a three-megapixel camera at the best image size setting, usually listed as Large or 3M, you'll be using all three million pixels, and you'll be able to print as large as 8×10 inches. However, if you set the image size to Medium or Small on that same three-megapixel camera, you'll be using only a portion of the maximum pixels, and you'll be limited in the size of the print you can make. The image quality (also sometimes referred to as *compression setting*) is usually listed as Fine or Superfine, Normal, and Basic. This setting tells the camera how you want the onboard processor to compress the image for storage on the memory card. Superfine or Fine means less compression than Normal or Basic. Generally, the less compression, the better the final image.

For scrapbooking and other craft projects, you should look for at least a three-megapixel camera and set it to the largest image size and best image quality possible on your particular camera. On the Nikon Coolpix 4200, a four-megapixel camera, this means setting the camera at the 4M (2272×1704) image size and the Fine image quality setting. On a Canon PowerShot S400, the equivalent optimal setting is Large (2272×1704) and S (Superfine). That way, you'll always be able to fill a page with your photograph. And if you need only a portion of that photo but want to make it a little larger to fit a certain design, you'll have the necessary resolution or pixels to do so.

Viewfinder

The *viewfinder* on both a film and a digital camera is a device you look through to choose your subject and frame your photo. An *optical viewfinder* is an eyepiece through which you see the actual photo you're taking. Most digital cameras have a built-in color screen on the back. On digital SLRs this screen is for reviewing pictures that have already been taken and for choosing the settings on the camera. On compact digital cameras, this LCD screen is also used for reviewing and making settings, but in addition can be used to view the image before you take the picture. You can frame your photos, just like an artist who holds his thumbs and index fingers to form a square and visualize the subject of his painting. In most situations, framing your photos this way works very well. However, in certain lighting conditions, such as bright sunlight, the images on the LCD screen can be difficult to see. Generally, it's best to select a compact digital camera with an optical viewfinder so you can frame your photos accurately in any light.

Digital cameras offer something we've never had before in photography: truly instant feedback. You click the shutter-release button, and you know by looking at the screen on the back of the camera if you got the shot you wanted. Talk about immediate gratification! Remember, a digital camera is a small computer with its own built-in *screen*. The camera's LCD screen can vary in size, and of course, bigger is nicer for viewing. However, keep in mind the screen is really only for making sure you got the shot, not for judging or fixing the quality of your photograph. You just want to be sure that everything or everyone who should be in the photo is in the photo. Use the digital zoom to enlarge it on the LCD. You'll know for sure if everyone's eyes are open! If they aren't, just take another shot or two. It's digital.

Shutter-Release Button

On most digital cameras, you press the *shutter-release button* halfway to allow the camera to focus and set the exposure. When you fully depress the shutter-release button, the camera takes the picture. It's a "two-step press." Pressing the shutter release on a digital camera initiates many electronic processes. Some digital cameras will have a longer *shutter-release lag*, which means the camera won't take the photo at the exact instant you press the button. The lag time varies with each type of camera. Many newer cameras have virtually no lag time. Check the camera specifications, and be sure to try the various cameras before you buy.

Flash

Flash Cancel
(Off)

Most digital cameras have some type of built-in *flash*. A flash is essential in many situations, and in other situations it can ruin a picture or prevent you from taking a picture altogether. Sometimes you don't want to use flash in low light because it will overly brighten your subject or look unnatural. Also, some museums may allow you to take pictures but not to use a flash. Museums control the amount of light to preserve the artwork. Since digital cameras can take better pictures in low light than film cameras, they're great for museums and other historic interior shots where you are allowed to take photographs. Make sure your digital camera has a setting for no flash.

Memory Cards

Both computers and digital cameras use *memory*. Computer memory is called RAM, *random access memory*. RAM gives the computer the power to use the software and allows the computer to store what you're working on temporarily, or until you turn off the computer. Digital cameras use *Flash* memory cards, which store photos until you intentionally erase them. Some digital cameras have limited built-in memory, however, choose a camera with a removable *memory card*. Memory cards are your "digital film." Compact Flash, Smart Media, SD Memory, XD Memory, and Memory Stick are different types of memory cards. Most digital SLRs use Compact Flash, the largest card in terms of physical size. Many compact digital cameras use SD Memory, a much smaller card.

It's the amount of memory in *megabytes (MB)* and not the physical size of the card that counts. The greater the number of megabytes, the more photographs the card can store, and the more expensive the card. Since you will want to take photos at the highest settings on your camera, get a card with lots of megabytes or enough to store at least 50 shots. A 128MB card in a four-megapixel point-and-shoot camera will store at least 55 shots. If you're just changing over from a film camera, that may seem like a lot. In the digital world it may not be enough. You will take more photos with a digital camera since you only print only the ones you like. Figure 4.7 and Figure 4.8 show some of the different types of memory cards available.

Figure 4.7 Some memory cards from Lexar Media   **Figure 4.8** Some memory cards from SanDisk

Unlike film, you can take a memory card out of the camera anytime, even if it isn't completely filled with photos. Once you've copied your photos to your computer or burned them to a CD, you can put the card back into the camera, turn on the camera, *format* the card, and continue taking pictures.

> **Note:** Always turn off the power to the camera before removing the memory card. Never pull the memory card out while the camera is on. You may lose the pictures that are on the card or damage the card.

Always *format* the card using the tools or set up menu in your camera. Formatting erases all the data or photos on the card, clears the card, and sets it up to record with your particular camera. Don't use the computer to erase photos or format the memory card, since it might not set the card to work with your particular camera, and it may cause problems with the card.

 Tip: Always *format* the memory card in the camera.

Batteries

All digital cameras need power. Unless you purchase a special power adapter and always use your camera near an electrical outlet, you'll be using *batteries*. Digital cameras tend to gobble up battery power, not only because of the computer that's processing the images but also because of the LCD on the back of the camera. Of course, most cameras have settings so you can turn down or off the LCD, but you need to review your photos to know if you got the shot, and you'll need to access the settings of the camera for various features. Besides, looking at the photo just after you shot it is so much fun!

Some digital cameras have their own proprietary battery and include the battery charger in the box. You can get a second proprietary battery to have a spare charged at all times. Others use regular, most often AA batteries. If your camera uses standard batteries, you can purchase a battery charger and rechargeable batteries. But you may want to take that one step further. Get rechargeable Nickel Metal Hydride (NiMh) batteries, rather than Nickel Cadmium (NiCd) batteries. NiMh is a type of rechargeable battery that doesn't have a "memory effect," meaning it won't remember if it was fully discharged, or used up, before it was recharged. You can recharge NiMh batteries many more times than other rechargeable batteries. Also, if your camera uses regular batteries, be sure to check the power requirements of the camera. The power rating will be indicated on the box or in the manual, and will look similar to 1.2v/1300mAh or 1.2v/2200mAh. Purchase a charger and rechargeable NiMh batteries of no less than that power rating. Otherwise, you'll run out of battery power quickly.

Camera Settings

Digital cameras are very good at capturing sharp and colorful images in most situations just by pressing the shutter in *automatic mode*. With digital SLRs and higher-end compact digital cameras, you can control all the settings individually in *manual mode*.

Macro

Some digital cameras include *macro* settings, so you can get very close to an object and make it full size (1:1), or almost full size, on the photograph. The macro setting is great for taking close-up nature shots, for taking pictures of objects for your scrapbooks, and for taking pictures of printed pages when you want the text to be legible in the photograph.

White Balance

Since cameras capture light, if you can tell the camera what kind of light is around you, the camera can do a much better job. This is referred to as setting the *white balance*.

Are you shooting in daylight on a sunny day or is it cloudy? Are you shooting in artificial light such as tungsten or neon? Better quality digital cameras will offer more white balance choices.

Underwater Housing

Some digital cameras have underwater housings available as an option, which allow you to take photos while swimming and even while SCUBA diving. And since digital cameras are better than film cameras in low-light situations, even deep-underwater photos will show the colors in the scene. The photo in Figure 4.9 was taken using a four-megapixel Canon S400 and an underwater housing. (The S410 in Figure 4.10 has replaced the S400 in Canon's digital camera line.)

Figure 4.9
Underwater photograph
© Jean-Marc Corredor

Figure 4.10
Canon PowerShot S410

Scenes

Nikon Coolpix and some other digital cameras provide special automatic *scene settings*. These set up the lighting and capture speeds for you. For example, Beach and Snow settings can help compensate for superbright scenes. Fireworks Show settings will allow you to easily take pictures of nighttime fireworks, and the Party/Indoor setting helps you take good pictures indoors with dim lighting. A camera such as the new Nikon Coolpix 4200 in Figure 4.11 is a perfect camera for most general photography and especially for scrapbooking. It not only takes sharp, clear, accurate color images, but it also includes the scene settings, which can make difficult shots easy for both new and more advanced photographers. And because of its ultra-small size, you can always have the camera with you to capture that unforgettable moment.

Figure 4.11
The Nikon Coolpix 4200 is easy to use and small enough to go with you everywhere.

Movie Mode

Many of the newer cameras will also include a *movie mode*, which can record short movies and sound. These are fun, but they tend to use up a lot of space on the memory card. Also, the quality of the individual frames isn't as good for printing as the normal photographic modes.

How you access any of these special features depends on the brand and model of digital camera. Most brands use similar icons to denote the information. Figure 4.12 shows some of the icons for various modes and settings.

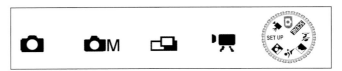

Figure 4.12
Typical digital camera icons

Figure 4.13 shows a chart of the special scene settings included on Nikon Coolpix cameras.

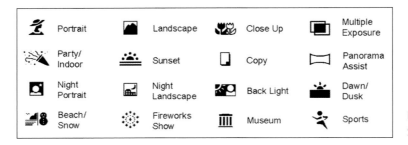

Figure 4.13
Sample Coolpix settings

Other Factors

All the bells and whistles available on a digital camera are only as good as they are easy to use. You access the different features of every camera the same way—that is, by using certain buttons, dials, or wheels sometimes in a sequence, and viewing the settings on the LCD. Try setting different modes on the camera while in the store.

Ergonomics will help you *use* the camera and must not be overlooked. How does the camera feel in your hands? Is it too small or too heavy for you? Does it feel balanced?

Know how you plan to use the camera. If you choose a very small camera, you can always have it with you ready to capture memories at any moment. If you choose a larger or "prosumer" camera, you'll have more settings and more control over different types of shots. If photography is your main hobby, you'll eventually have both types, a larger one for your planned and artistic photos and a smaller one for everyday snapshots.

Digital Camera Shopping List

☑ **Traditional camera manufacturer brand**: Pick a brand that's known for cameras.

☑ **Compact digital camera or digital SLR:** Choose a camera you'll use. Small compact digital cameras are good to keep with you all the time. Digital SLRs offer many more features.

☑ **Features and your budget:** Pick the features you really want. Some may not be important to you.

☑ **Megapixels:** Three to four megapixels is sufficient for scrapbooking.

☑ **Viewfinder:** Choose a camera with an optical viewfinder (an eyepiece to frame your pictures).

☑ **Flash/No Flash Controls:** Choose a camera with flash control and easy access to these controls.

☑ **Zoom:** Optical zoom should be 3× or greater. Don't consider the digital zoom factor.

☑ **Batteries:** Get a battery charger and NiMh batteries or a spare proprietary (camera brand) battery.

☑ **Memory card:** Choose a large capacity, large number of megabyte card. Get spare cards.

☑ **Memory card reader:**Choose a reader for multiple types of memory.

☑ **Camera bag:** Look for padding for the LCD.

☑ **Tripod or monopod:** Find a tripod that sets up quickly and easily and that's stable with your camera. Make sure the camera has a tripod socket and that the tripod fits, or get an adapter.

The Care and Feeding of Your Digital Camera

Use the following to-do list for keeping your camera in working condition and for protecting your investment:

Protect the lens and LCD   On traditional cameras, the most fragile item is the lens. On digital cameras, you must also protect the LCD. Get a good case. Go to a camera store to test for size, or try Lowepro.com, the home site for Lowepro camera bags. They have a page of "camera matrices" where they match many camera models with appropriate bags in the Lowepro line. Replacing a broken LCD could cost more than some cameras.

Protect the lens on small point-and-shoot cameras by turning the camera off when you aren't using it and putting on the lens cap if it has one. Most digital cameras have settings that will automatically turn off the camera after a specified period of time.

Keep on top of your batteries and chargers   Keep your batteries charged and have a spare set with you, especially when traveling. Most chargers included with digital cameras work on both 110 and 220 voltage, so they work on foreign current. To charge your batteries in other countries, you should need only the proper adapter plug for that country. When you purchase a separate battery charger, make sure it says "input: 100–220V AC 50–60Hz" so you can use it internationally.

Get spare memory cards   Purchase at least one spare memory card—more if you're traveling. The larger the number of megabytes on the card, the more pictures you can take on each card.

Consider a tripod   Consider getting a *tripod* if your camera has a tripod socket. Low-light shots and macro shots require a steady hand when holding the camera. Tripods or *monopods*, the single-leg type, make this much easier.

Setting Up Your Digital Camera for the First Time

The easiest way to learn to use your digital camera and all its wonderful features is to follow these steps:

1. If the camera comes with a "Getting Started" CD, view it first.

2. Follow the instructions on the "Getting Started" card.

3. Fully charge the batteries, or use fresh standard batteries.

4. Insert a memory card.

5. Sit with the camera and instruction manual for about an hour, *read the manual* and try every feature! More than any other peripheral, a digital camera has so much in such a small package that the settings and where to find them aren't always obvious.

Start with the camera setup, setting the time and date and the personalized sounds you'd like the camera to make, and then format the memory card. Take lots of photos. Try all the modes and scene settings. Take pictures at each setting to see what your camera can do. Remember, you can reformat the memory card and recharge the batteries, so nothing is wasted.

6. Finally, always remember to format the memory card in the camera and not in the computer.

Getting Your Photos onto Your Computer

With film, you take the roll out of the camera and take it or mail it to a photo lab. With digital, you have many more options, and each method has its own benefits.

Most cameras include a cable to connect the camera directly to your computer. Sometimes, you can connect the camera directly to an inkjet printer. Direct connections work well but are a huge drain on the batteries. Some inkjet printers have slots where you can insert the memory cards and print your photos. You can also take the memory card to a photo kiosk or other direct printing device at a local store to have your photos printed. Both these methods work well; however, they limit your ability to fix and crop the images. Being able change your photos before you print them is the biggest advantage of digital photography.

Using a *card reader* is the easiest way to transfer the images from the memory card into your own computer. Figure 4.14 and Figure 4.15 show *multicard readers* from Lexar and SanDisk.

We recommend multicard readers, since they're capable of reading various types of memory cards. Although your own digital camera may use one type of memory card, having the ability to read other types can be useful, especially when working with family photos and family members whose cameras may use a different type of card. You simply plug the card reader into a USB port on your computer. When you insert a memory card, it shows up on your desktop as an external drive. You can them copy the images onto your computer's hard drive for later viewing, fixing, and storage. To remove the memory card from the reader, you select it and click the Safely Remove Hardware icon on your taskbar on a PC or just drag the card icon to the trash on a Mac. Then pull the card out of the reader.

If you have a laptop computer with a PC or PCMCIA slot (a thin, two-inch wide slot on the side of the computer), you can also use a PC card adapter such as the ones from Lexar and SanDisk in Figure 4.16 and Figure 4.17. You put the memory card into the adapter and then slip the whole combination into the slot on your notebook. Adapter cards function just like an external reader from that point.

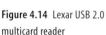

Figure 4.14 Lexar USB 2.0 multicard reader

Figure 4.15 SanDisk Image-mate reader/writer

Figure 4.16 Lexar PC card adapter

Figure 4.17 SanDisk PC card adapter

Once you've fixed your photographs with Photoshop Elements, you can print directly from your computer. Or use the card reader to copy the images from your computer back onto the memory card and take the fixed photos on the card to be printed elsewhere.

One Last Thought...

The first digital cameras that worked with a home computer were released in 1994 and were less than one megapixel. The choices were few, and the ways to get your photos printed were limited. Today, digital cameras are affordable with many choices in price, brands, and options. And they can produce excellent-quality images, often better than film photographs. You can take all the photos you want, never miss that memorable moment, and actually save on processing and printing costs. You'll have more and better photos to put in your scrapbooks and heritage books. It's time to shoot digital.

Scanners Aren't Scary

5

A digital camera is the best tool for recording your memories. A scanner, however, is the most creative tool for all crafts, especially scrapbooking. More important, a scanner can help you restore as well as archive older memorabilia and photos. Yet scanners scare some people. Why? Perhaps it's all those numbers associated with scanning. The numbers are important, but you don't need to do any math. First you have to find the right scanner for your needs, and then the rest of the steps will be easy.

Chapter Contents

What to look for in a scanner
Creating scanner-computer connections
Scanning software
Planning your scan
The care and feeding of your Scanner

What to Look for in a Scanner

Think of a scanner as a box with a glass top. Inside the box, you'll find a lightbulb and a series of tiny digital cameras called *image sensors*. The cameras take a picture of whatever is on the glass. These image sensors are either sitting on a carriage that moves down the scanning area or sitting at the back of the scanner box and capturing the image bounced by mirrors that move along the track. Either way, something is moving in the box when the scanner is scanning. The scanner digitizes the image by breaking up what it sees into dots. The scanning software in your computer then uses the digital information to create the image you see on your screen.

Why talk about the parts of the scanner? You need to be aware of the hardware parts, how a scanner works, and how to take care of it in order to keep getting the best possible scans.

The following are several types of scanners:

Drum scanners　These are large and expensive and are used by professional design firms.

Film scanners　These only scan transparencies (Figure 5.1)

Note: A *transparency* is film, either a negative or a slide. Some software will refer to a slide as a *positive transparency* and a negative as a *negative transparency*.

Figure 5.1
Nikon Coolscan V ED film scanner
© Nikon Inc. All rights
reserved.

Flatbed scanners　These scan *reflective* pieces, meaning photographs, pages, paintings, or three-dimensional objects.

Flatbed scanners with transparency adapters　These can scan both reflective pieces such as photographs as well as film. A *transparency adapter* included with some flatbed scanners is a special top or separate piece you use to scan slides or negatives.

A flatbed scanner with a transparency adapter is the most useful and affordable type of scanner for scrapbooking. Although a simple flatbed scanner is less expensive and will do the job for most photos or solid objects, if you ever plan on scanning a negative or slide, you should definitely consider a scanner with a transparency adapter. Figure 5.2, Figure 5.3, and Figure 5.4 show several brands and models.

Figure 5.2 Microtek ScanMaker i320 flatbed scanner

Figure 5.3 Canon CanoScan 9900F flatbed scanner

Figure 5.4 Epson Perfection 2580 flatbed scanner

All-in-ones   Also called *multifunction printers*, all-in-ones come with a built-in printer. They can scan, print, and even photocopy. You can use multifunction printers for scrapbooking projects as long as the built-in printer is specified as a *photo printer* and as long as the scanner includes a transparency unit. Figure 5.5 shows an Epson all-in-one scanner, printer, and copier. This model even includes a memory card reader.

Figure 5.5
Epson Stylus PhotoRX
500 all-in-one

Bit-Depth

Bit-depth refers to the range of tones or colors a scanner can capture. One bit is one black or white dot. Eight bits of information will give you a range of grays from white to black. Since color scanners capture color as three colors—RGB (red, green, blue)—the minimum bit-depth for a color scanner is 3 multiplied by 8 bits, or 24 (see Figure 5.6). The bit-depth on a color scanner will always be divisible by 3. A larger number for the bit-depth means the scanner is capable of recording a larger *tonal range*, or more variances of each color. This is especially important for skin tones in your snapshots. You may not be able to see the differences on your monitor, but a higher bit-depth scan will give more information for the computer to work with when you adjust or change the colors in your image. A good-quality color scanner for scrapbooking will have at least 36 to 48 for the bit-depth.

1 Bit

8 Bit

24 Bit

Figure 5.6
Bit-depth

DMax

DMax is the maximum optical density that the scanner can record, with 4.0 being a theoretical solid black. This number refers to the amount of detail the scanner can capture in the shadows and highlights of a photo. The higher the number, the blacker the blacks, and the greater the amount of detail will be visible in the scanned image. High DMax is most important when scanning negatives and slides.

A good-quality color scanner for scrapbooking will have a DMax of at least 3.2 in its technical specifications. If you plan to scan negatives or slides using a transparency adapter, look for a scanner with a DMax of 3.6 or higher.

Resolution

The dpi (which stands for *dots per inch*) listed on the scanner box describes the capabilities of the scanner or the amount of information that the scanner can record. The resolution for a scanner is shown as two numbers, such as 2400×4800 dpi or 4800×2400 dpi, depending on the manufacturer. The larger number refers to the *subscan*, or the number of half steps per inch that the scanning "cameras" move vertically during the scan. The smaller number refers to the *optical resolution*, or the maximum number of dots per inch that the scanner records horizontally. The *optical resolution* is the important number when choosing a scanner. The greater the optical resolution number, the more data the scanner can record and the more you can enlarge what you scan.

You also may see the term *interpolated resolution*. Interpolated resolution isn't true optical resolution and shouldn't be considered when comparing scanners. *Interpolated* means the scanning software is inventing some pixels between the existing pixels in the original image. The resulting image won't be as clear as the original.

A good-quality color scanner for scrapbooking will have at least 2400 dpi for the optical resolution (or at least 2400 for the smaller of the two dpi numbers in the manufacturer's description).

Scanner Bed

The scanner bed is the area on the scanner glass that can be scanned at one time. Most flatbed scanners have at least a letter-size or slightly larger scanning bed. Others can scan a legal size page at 8½×14 inches. Professional flatbed scanners can scan a page 12.2×17.2 inches at one time and are great for scanning full-size scrapbook pages, but these scanners are very large and expensive.

Note: You can scan a scrapbook page that's 12×12 inches with a letter-size scanner and Adobe Photoshop Elements using the technique described in Chapter 13 of this book.

Shopping List for Scanners

The following is a shopping list for buying a scanner:

- ☑ **Flatbed scanner**: Get one with a transparency adapter.
- ☑ **Resolution:** You'll need a minimum 2400×4800 dpi. (The smaller number is the true optical resolution and the one that counts.)
- ☑ **DMax:** You'll need a minimum 3.2 to 3.6 DMax.
- ☑ **Bit-Depth:** You'll need a minimum 36 bit-depth.
- ☑ **Photo repair technology and color restoration software:** Look for a scanner with built-in photo repair and color restoration technology such as: Digital ICE, FARE, PictuRescue, ColoRescue, or Easy Photo Fix.
- ☑ **Cable:** USB 1, USB 2, or FireWire. (Some scanner manufacturers supply a cable.)
- ☑ **Image-editing software:** Adobe Photoshop Elements.
- ☑ **Other supplies:** You may need clear plastic wrap, a photo bulb blower, a soft lint-free cloth, *and* a large piece of black fabric (for scanning three-dimensional items and 12x12 pages).

Creating Scanner-Computer Connections

The scanner needs to communicate with the computer, both by hardware and software.

Cables

The hardware connection determines the type of cable you'll need to connect the two machines. Serial, SCSI, FireWire, USB 1, and USB 2 are some of the connections types. SCSI stands for small computer systems interface and USB stands for universal serial bus. SCSI is an older technology. Today, Firewire and USB are much more common and convenient. See Figure 5.7.

Figure 5.7
USB and FireWire cables

Software Drivers and TWAIN

The computer uses a software driver to control the scanner, just as it uses a different driver to control the printer. Unlike the printer, however, the scanner needs to communicate with the computer to describe what it sees on the scanner glass.

Scanner manufacturers include drivers and communication, or *interface*, modules on the installation CD. Many scanner manufacturers use an interface technology called TWAIN. (The definitions of TWAIN as a name or as an acronym vary.) Although this technology is often used between a scanner or even a digital camera and the image processing software in the computer, other scanner manufacturers supply a proprietary interface module with their own brand name. When you first set up your scanner, you install the appropriate drivers and interface modules for your operating system. So, for instance, if you're using Windows XP, you'll need the current driver for XP.

 Note: Whenever you update your computer's operating system or get a new computer, be sure to check the scanner manufacturer's website and download the latest scanner drivers for your specific operating system.

Some scanners include a software package that allows for one-button scanning. One-button scanning means you can place an item on the scanner glass and press a button on the front of the scanner to start scanning the image. However, for scrapbooking, it's best to use Adobe Photoshop Elements to control the scan.

The Scanner Dialog Box

When you are ready to scan, launch Adobe Photoshop Elements. Select File > Import and choose the name of your scanner's interface module or TWAIN, whichever is listed. You should see a *dialog box* with some scanner settings. Figure 5.8 and Figure 5.9 show the dialog boxes of two brands of scanners.

Each scanner brand has a slightly different dialog box. You may even have a choice of modes, such as Standard, Home, Office, or Professional mode, each with different settings. As a general rule, you indicate what type of item you're scanning and how you intend to use it. In other words, are you scanning a photo or a negative? Are you going to use the scanned image at the same size as or smaller than the original, or will you make it larger for your project?

Since the scanner dialog boxes differ from model to model, the following explanations are general. It's always best to check the instruction manual for your particular scanner.

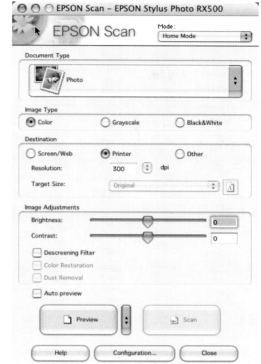

Figure 5.8

A Microtek scanner dialog box

Figure 5.9

An Epson scanner dialog box

Source image or original   Some scanners give options of *Photo* (also called Reflective) or *Transparency*. A transparency can be a negative, (also called negative film) or a slide (also called positive film). If you're scanning a negative or a slide, choose a setting in the dialog box to match. For every other type of scan, including three-dimensional items, choose Photo (or Reflective) when scanning for a scrapbook page.

Target image   Some scanners ask only about the kind of output you want. Mark the option that indicates color or the True Color option. You want the scanner to make a color scan of whatever is on the scanner glass. Even black-and-white photos and documents such as diplomas should be scanned as color images for scrapbook and craft projects. A color scan has more digital information in the file. The additional data from the color scan will make it easier to fix or change the image in Adobe Photoshop Elements, and you'll end up with a better image for your project.

> **Note:** You can turn any color image into a black-and-white image using Adobe Photoshop Elements as described in Chapter 9 of this book.

Target size   The target size means the final width and height you want to print or save your image. It may be 4×5 inches, 5×7 inches, or any size that fits your design.

Resolution   Resolution and target size are related. For scrapbooking and craft projects, you want the scanned image to have a resolution of 300 ppi, with the width and height dimensions to fit your project. For example, if you scan a 4×6 photograph that you intend to reprint at 4×6 inches, scan at 300 ppi. With a slide, the scan area is very small, actually less than 1×1½ inches. If you want a 4×6 print from a slide, you would scan the slide at four times the resolution, or four times 300 ppi, which is 1200 ppi.

Note: You *don't* have to do any math. Most new scanners make setting the resolution easy. You select the *resolution* as 300 ppi and set the target size to the dimensions you want for your project. The scanner software does the math.

dpi and ppi: 300 Is the Magic Number

You'll see both dpi and ppi in various scanning dialog boxes and in Adobe Photoshop Elements. dpi refers to the *dots per inch*. ppi refers to the *pixels per inch*. Sometimes the terms are also used synonymously in instruction books, making it even more confusing. With some scanner software, you select the pixels-per-inch resolution you want the scanner to scan. With other scanner software, you determine the dots-per-inch resolution you need to print the final image. Either way, 300 is the best number to use.

Scanning Software

Without software, scanners like computers are just expensive boxes with electronic parts and wires. The software application is the magic that turns whatever you put on the scanner glass into an image you can see on your monitor.

Built-in Photo Restoration Technology and Software

Some of the newest scanners can actually repair tears, remove dust and scratches, and improve colors as they scan photographs by using a specific hardware technology and/or special built-in software. These scanners can save a scrapbooker many hours of initial repair work, especially when scanning older heritage photographs, leaving more time for creativity and page design with Adobe Photoshop Elements. Digital ICE is one name for this technology and FARE, PictuRescue, ColoRescue, and Easy Photo Fix are some of the brand names for built-in photo restoration software.

Software for Scanning Text

If you're scanning a page of text or a document in which you want to change the words, you'll need OCR (optical character recognition) software to "recognize" the page as text before you can use word processing software to edit the text. If you're scanning a document or text to place directly in your scrapbook page, you need only image-editing software such as Adobe Photoshop Elements.

Image-Editing Software: Adobe Photoshop Elements

When you scan photographs, documents, backgrounds, or any objects, the result is an image file. Using image-editing software, you can correct and print that image file and save it for archiving. You can change the size, adjust the colors, remove red-eye, crop the image for shape, and do much more.

Although many image-editing and scrapbooking software packages are on the market, Adobe Photoshop Elements is the most complete application for scrapbooking, home photography, and crafts.

Adobe Photoshop Elements is the little brother of the premier image-editing software, Adobe Photoshop, used by professional photographers and graphic designers throughout the world. Elements has every feature a scrapbooker and home photographer would use from the full version of Photoshop, even a few more, with simplified steps and a How To menu always open on the screen. You can use Adobe Photoshop Elements to stylize journaling, create page toppers, and design borders, even complete backgrounds. You can fix and crop photographs or design an entire page with the computer.

Planning Your Scan

You need to know the destination before you plan the journey. The same applies to scanning. What are you going to do with the image file you get from scanning? Are you only going to e-mail it? Are you going to print it? What size print do you want? Make a plan, and then set up and scan.

Step 1: Calibrate your monitor   Each monitor shows colors differently. Calibrating the monitor helps it display the image with reasonable color accuracy.

Run Adobe Gamma on a PC or use the Display Calibrator Assistant in the Mac System Preferences.

For more accuracy, use a colorimeter, as described in detail in the Appendix.

Step 2: Clean the scanner glass   Dust and fingerprints on the glass will be scanned along with the photo or other object, and they're difficult to remove from the digital image.

First, use a bulb blower to blow off any particles or dust. Dust particles can scratch the scanner glass if they get rubbed into the surface.

Second, use a soft, lint-free cloth to polish the glass. Microfiber lens or eyeglass cloths work well.

If the glass has something stuck to it, use a little rubbing alcohol on a soft cloth and wipe the glass. Never spray or pour the alcohol directly on the scanner glass. Make sure to let the alcohol evaporate completely before turning on the scanner.

Step 3: Clean the item you're scanning   The scanner will scan everything it sees on the glass.

Use a bulb blower to blow off any dust on the photograph, negative, or slide. Clean other items as necessary.

Step 4: Align the item on the scanner glass   Straighten and align the objects or photos on the scanner glass. This saves lots of time and frustration straightening them later.

Using a small ruler or straight edge on the glass can be helpful.

Step 5: Determine what you're scanning   In the scanner dialog box, tell the scanner what's on the scanner glass. Is it a photo, a slide, a negative?

Step 6: Determine your target size In the scanner dialog box, tell the scanner what width and height you want the final image.

Step 7: Scan at 300 ppi In the scanner dialog box, set the resolution (dpi or ppi depending on the scanner model) to 300. See Figure 5.10 and Figure 5.11.

 Note: The best resolution for an image for printing on an ink-jet printer and for storing on CD is 300 dpi or ppi.

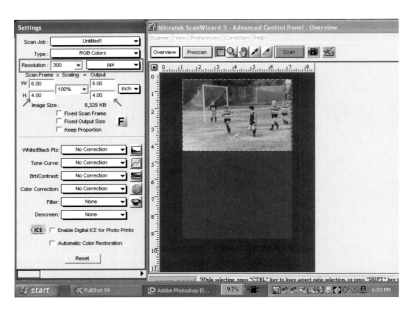

Figure 5.10
Scanning a photo at 300 ppi on a Microtek Scan-Maker i320 scanner

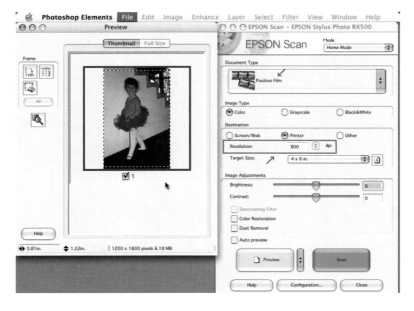

Figure 5.11
Scanning a photo at 300 dpi on an Epson Stylus PhotoRX 500 all-in-one

Understanding file size and its relation to computer memory (RAM) and hard drive space.

Digital image files can be large. You want to scan images so they will end up at 300 ppi with the dimensions you need for your scrapbook page or other project.

The industry standard and the ideal resolution (ppi) for storing or printing image files is 300 ppi.

An image that's 8×10 inches at 300 ppi creates a file that's more than 20 megabytes (MB) in size. An image that's 12×12 inches at 300 ppi creates a file that's more than 37MB.

The computer needs a large amount of RAM to work on or *process* such large files.

The computer uses memory (RAM) to process photos and other files. RAM stands for Random Access Memory. Think of RAM as the working space available on a table or desk in your office. The bigger the desk, the more room you have to layout your project, and the larger the project you can work on at one time.

The computer hard drive is different. The hard drive is like a file cabinet where you store files. The larger the file cabinet, or the larger the hard drive, the more finished files you can store.

You need enough working space to process the files and you need storage space to store them when they are finished or when you shut off the computer.

Adobe recommends a minimum of 256 MB of RAM to work with Photoshop Elements. However, with scrapbooking files, you will probably want more RAM to scan and work on scrapbook pages and page parts.

If your computer slows down or stops when you're working on image files, it probably doesn't have enough RAM. Try closing any other open files or applications to free up more RAM memory for Photoshop Elements.

Installing more RAM is the best solution.

If that isn't possible, you can scan and set all the files you use for scrapbooking at 200 ppi or even 150 ppi, but never lower. The image quality will be degraded slightly, but it may not be that noticeable depending on your inkjet printer. This is especially true of backgrounds and clip art.

Lowering the resolution (ppi) of the files while leaving the width and height the same, reduces the file size and thus the amount of memory (RAM) required for the computer to work on the images. In any case, keep all the files you use including the background, clip art, titles, and photographs set to the same resolution (ppi) when assembling complete pages in the computer.

Another option, if you can't add more RAM to your computer, is to create the backgrounds, text, and other embellishments at 150 ppi, always using the width and height you want for the final page and parts, and print these separately. Scan, store, and print the photographs individually as 300 ppi image files. Assemble your scrapbook page as in traditional scrapbooking, gluing the photographs onto the rest of the digitally designed and printed page.

The Care and Feeding of Your Scanner

The scanner is an amazing tool. However, you should follow certain rules so that it can perform the way it was designed to do.

Rule 1: Put the scanner on a solid surface   The table supporting the scanner must not move as the scanner scans.

Rule 2: Always clean the scanner glass before scanning   Use a bulb blower and soft cloth on the glass each time before you scan.

 Note: Never use household cleaning solutions on computer equipment. Many cleaning solutions contain ammonia or other solvents that can damage the computer parts.

Rule 3: Clean the photo or item you're scanning   Use a bulb blower to get rid of dust on photos, negatives, or slides.

Rule 4: Don't put anything on top of the scanner   Don't use the scanner as a bookshelf or a table, and never lean on the scanner lid (Figure 5.12).

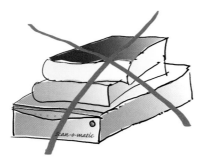

Figure 5.12
Don't use the scanner as a place to stack your stuff.

Rule 5: Always turn off the power and lock the scanner before moving it   Most scanners have a locking switch or locking screw to prevent the internal parts from moving during shipping. When you first get your scanner, unlocking the scanner is the first step in setting it up. If you need to move the scanner later, first turn off the power to the scanner and then lock the scanner.

Rule 6: Protect the scanner glass   If you're scanning something that could scratch the glass, such as medals, or something that's sticky or wet, such as candy or flowers, cover the glass first with clear plastic wrap. If you're scanning something that could leak, make sure you use plastic wrap on the glass and over the entire scanner bed. The scanner glass isn't sealed, and the liquid could run into the mechanism inside the box.

Rule 7: Keep the underside of the scanner lid clean   Cover the top of sticky items with plastic wrap or a clean sheet of paper (Figure 5.13).

Figure 5.13
Be sure to use plastic wrap to protect your scanner from messy scanning material.

Rule 8: Don't let the scanner see the light in the room   You want the scanner to see only the objects on the glass. When you put three-dimensional objects, such as candy, crayons, flowers, jewelry, or even a book on the scanner glass, you probably won't be able to completely close the scanner lid. With the items to be scanned in place on the glass, close the lid lightly. Then cover the closed scanner with a large piece of black fabric to keep out the surrounding light, like photographers used to do with old-fashioned cameras (Figure 5.14).

Figure 5.14
Keep out the surrounding light.

Note: To scan a three-dimensional item, first cover the glass with clear plastic wrap. Place the three-dimensional items on the plastic. Close the scanner lid only as far as it will go. Cover the entire scanner with a large black cloth.

One Last Thought…

A scanner is a tool for the creative imagination. Photographs and negatives aren't the only items you can scan. Scan children's artwork and valuable documents, and create a digital copy to be printed, saved, and stored. Scan three-dimensional items such as decorative pins, ribbons, and medals. Make them part of your pages, and store the originals separately. Scan a piece of lace, crayons, or candies, and create your own backgrounds for your pages. You can scan an entire finished page using the technique described later in this book. Then reprint the digital page at various sizes for family and friends, and archive the original file on CD media. Scanners aren't scary; they're magical.

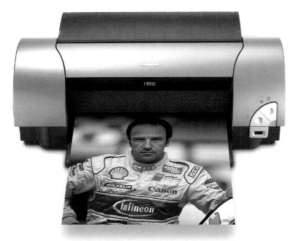

Ink-Jet Printers: A Primer

Digital technology is changing the way we do many things, including waiting for prints when film is developed. You can see the photos from a digital camera as soon as you take them. With an inkjet printer, you can have prints almost as quickly. Color ink-jet printers bring the convenience of printing photos into the home and office at an affordable price.

Whether you design projects on a computer, scan old photos for archiving, or simply take digital photos, you'll eventually want a printed version of that image.

6

Chapter Contents

All types of printers
Choosing an ink-jet printer for scrapbooking
The care and feeding of your ink-jet printer
Printing with photo services

All Types of Printers

Printers run the gamut from handheld and desktop printers to large commercial printing presses. The one feature all color printers have in common is the basic ink set of *CMYK* (which stands for cyan, magenta, yellow, and black). Cyan, magenta, and yellow are the basic colors of transparent inks used in printing to reproduce all the colors of an image. Black is added in most printing to increase contrast and to get a truer black. See Figure 6.1.

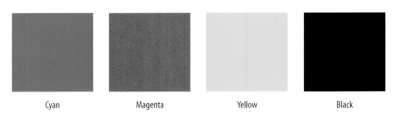

| Cyan | Magenta | Yellow | Black |

Figure 6.1
Cyan, magenta, yellow, and black are the colors of a printer's basic ink set.

For photo printing and scrapbooking purposes, an ink-jet printer is going to be your likely choice. Ink-jet printers reproduce an image on a page by spraying tiny drops of liquid ink onto paper. The basic ink-jet technologies vary depending on the manufacturer. Think of an ink-jet as a squirt gun. The print head on the front of the "gun" has many tiny nozzles that spray ink. The technology used to "pull the trigger" and spray the ink can include bubble, thermal, and piezoelectric. In a bubble-jet or thermal bubble printer, such as those from Canon and Hewlett-Packard (HP), heat forces the ink out of the print head nozzles. In a piezoelectric ink-jet such as an Epson printer, electrical pulses cause the ink reservoir walls to push inward, pushing the ink through the nozzles and onto the paper.

Ink-jet printers are relatively inexpensive and can print on a variety of paper types. They're accurate and easy to use. The hardest part is deciding which of the many features available are important for your projects.

You may want to know a little bit about other types of printers, such as professional digital photographic printers used by many camera stores, some warehouse stores, and online photo printing services. Two basic types exist, and for scrapbookers the difference is important.

One type of professional digital photographic printer prints your photos almost instantly, as soon as you put your digital media into a slot. These generally use ink-jet or dye sublimation technology. The prints look like photos but usually offer only one paper choice and limited print sizes. The print longevity from these commercial instant printers varies depending on the printer and paper.

The other type of professional photographic printer prints digital images onto photographic, light-sensitive paper using a process similar to the traditional film processing known as *silver halide*. When you send or take your digital images to companies with this type of printer, you'll have to wait from an hour to a couple of days for the prints. Generally you will have a choice of glossy or photo-matte paper and a choice of sizes from traditional photographs to poster-sized prints. The prints you receive are actual photographs with the same archival qualities as traditional film prints. PhotoWorks.com and Adobe Photoshop Services both use this type of professional digital photographic printer.

Other printers you may have used in an office or seen in the store include laser and color laser printers. They use fine powder black and color toners, a laser beam, static electricity, and heat to transfer the toner and fuse it onto the paper. They're very fast but can be expensive. Although laser prints are less prone to fading, they often don't produce an image with true photographic quality, so even if you have access to one, your ink-jet is a better bet.

Dye sublimation printers use CMYK dyes on individual layers of plastic transfer film, and they transfer the images to special papers with a heat process. Consumer dye sublimation printers print excellent photographic images but usually no larger than a postcard or 4×6 inches. They're fun and quick but limiting for scrapbookers. And the cost per print is often higher than other solutions.

Solid ink printers and thermal wax printers use wax ink sticks or wax ribbons to apply colors on the page. Both these types of printers are used mostly for business applications and for printing on transparencies; again, the images don't look like traditional photographs. Dot-matrix, or impact printers, aren't color printers and are used mostly for business printing on multipage forms.

At the far end of the spectrum is the printing press, a large professionally operated machine that's used to print books, magazines, newspapers, and anything that requires numerous identical copies.

Choosing an Ink-Jet Printer for Scrapbooking

Basic color ink-jet printers today include the four inks—CMYK. Photo ink-jet printers may include extra colors of ink, a photo black, or other special photo inks. The added inks increase the range of tones and contrast and help the ink-jet print look just like a traditional photograph—sometimes better. Unless you're going to print only text, you should look for a printer that's labeled a photo printer. In addition to the inks, the spray patterns and droplet sizes of photo ink-jet printers are calculated to resemble the continuous tones of traditional photographs.

DPI and Droplet Size

The specifications of ink-jet printers list the maximum printer resolution in dpi and the minimum ink droplet size in *picoliters* (or millionths of a liter). The quality of the ink-jet print depends on the resolution, the size of the droplets, and the precision with which the dots are placed on the paper. Ink-jet printer resolution isn't the same as image resolution. Printer resolution refers to the number of dots per square inch, or dpi, the printer can print. (Image resolution refers to the number of pixels per inch that make up the image in the digital file.) Each printed dot consists of many droplets of ink, sprayed onto the paper in precise patterns called halftoning. The term comes from the printing industry, where a dot of black ink makes black, and dots half the size and slightly spread apart give the illusion of gray. The same applies to colors. A color as you see it on a commercially printed piece actually consists of many tiny dots of different colors set in certain patterns. These patterns are what allow you to see continuous tone color. Try looking at a colored area of a magazine page using a 10-power magnifying glass. You will probably see dots of various colors, rather than one solid color.

To get a sharp, photo-quality ink-jet print, your printer should be capable of printing at least 1440 dpi up to 2880 dpi. Some printer models offer higher resolutions, putting more dots on the paper or optimizing the resolution to be the equivalent of more dots.

The droplet size is equally important to the image's clarity. The smaller the droplet, the better the detail and the smoother the color gradations will appear in the printed photo. Droplet size is expressed in *picoliters*. A 4-picoliter droplet will produce excellent photo-quality prints. Some of today's printers have droplet sizes of 1.5 and 2 picoliters, offering even better quality details and tones.

Ink Colors and Cartridge Type

The first photo ink-jet printers had one cartridge filled with black ink and another that contained all the color inks. Today, photo printers not only offer more inks, they also may have individual color cartridges (see Figure 6.2). In general, individual ink tanks are more economical, since you replace only the cartridge of the color that's empty. This is especially true when printing designs and page parts, which may use much more of one color than another. In printing color photographs, individual color usage may be more equal. Ink usage totally depends on the kind of images and photos that are printed.

Figure 6.2
Individual ink cartridges

Printer manufacturers suggest a numbers of prints that their cartridges can produce. However, the calculations are always based on one type of paper and one type of image. Since you'll most likely print a variety of images on a variety of sizes and papers for scrapbooking projects, the numbers aren't really useful for judging your own ink usage.

To create a wide tonal range, many manufacturers have added inks to the CMYK standards. Light cyan and light magenta help create smoother color transitions, especially in the lighter colors and some skin tones. Adding light black or gray ink helps create more neutral blacks and variations in the shadows. Adding red and green inks can help expand the color gamut, or the range of colors that can be produced by the printer. Some printers have photo optimizer cartridges to help keep the gloss on glossy paper prints.

Ink Type

If you're concerned about your photos fading over time, you'll want to pay attention to the type of ink in your ink-jet printer. Most desktop ink-jet printers use a dye-based ink set. A few such as the Epson Stylus Photo 2200, shown in Figure 6.3, use pigment-based inks.

Figure 6.3
Epson Stylus Photo 2200

Dye-based inks offer a wider color range, or color gamut, while pigment-based inks have a higher lightfast and gasfast rating—but only when used on specific papers. The lightfast rating refers to how long a print will resist fading when exposed to indoor light. The gasfast rating refers to how long a print will resist fading when exposed to air pollutants.

Maximum Print Size

Desktop ink-jets can print images on various-sized papers, from 4×6 inches to 13×19 inches. A few printers print only the small photo sizes. Others can print borderless photos, the images without white borders, on all standard photo-sized papers, such as 4×6, 5×7, and 8×10. For scrapbooking and craft projects, it's best to choose a printer that can print on letter-sized paper as well as smaller sizes. The large-format printers, such as the Epson 1280 or 2200 and the Canon i9100 or and i9900 (shown in Figure 6.4), are useful if you want to print an entire 12×12 page, an 11×14 photo, or a 13×19 poster.

Figure 6.4
The Canon i9900 prints up
to 13 inches wide.

CHAPTER 6: INK-JET PRINTERS: A PRIMER ■

Special Features

For scrapbooking, you'll also want to consider the following factors when choosing your printer:

Printing speed   Manufacturers advertise the pages printed per minute. For photos and scrapbooks, this isn't as important as the quality of the print.

Noise   Noise levels of ink-jet printers vary. If this is important to you, go to a store and listen to several models as they print.

Size   A printer may fit onto a specific shelf or area; however, it may not be able to print from that space if you can't open the output tray or the paper support.

Roll paper   Printers that print on roll paper are useful when making panoramic prints; however, getting the curl out of the paper can be difficult.

Printing to CD and DVD media   Some printers such as the Epson R300 and the Epson R800, shown in Figure 6.5, can print images or identifying information directly on the surface of CD and DVD media that's ink-jet printable. (These printers don't burn the data on the media.)

Figure 6.5
The Epson Stylus Photo R800 can print an image directly onto CD or DVD media that's ink-jet printable.

Direct printing from a digital camera   Many newer ink-jet photo printers have a connector for attaching a digital camera directly to the printer using a USB cable. Although this may seem convenient, using the camera with a direct connection will quickly drain the camera batteries. In addition, without a computer and monitor, you can judge your photos only on the tiny camera screen or the LCD on some printers. Also, printing directly from the camera means you may print some undesirable photos, wasting ink and paper. And printing the photos as shot prevents you from enhancing or fixing them with Adobe Photoshop Elements.

Built-in memory card slots   Although built-in memory card slots have some of the same disadvantages as direct printing, they're useful in different ways. A built-in memory card slot can serve as a card reader when the printer is attached to your computer. Use it to *download* the photos from the card to your computer. After working on the files with Adobe Photoshop Elements, you can upload the finished image files back to the memory card. Then print your images directly from the card while freeing your computer to continue working on other projects. Figure 6.6 shows the memory card slots on the Epson Stylus Photo RX500 and the HP Photosmart 7960.

Figure 6.6 Memory card slots on the Epson Stylus Photo RX500 (left) and HP Photosmart 7960 (right)

Multiple paper paths Printers that offer multiple paper-feeding options can be convenient. Some models allow you to have different sizes and types of paper loaded at the same time. With the touch of a button, you can print 4×6 photos and then letter-sized images, without changing paper in the printer. The HP Photosmart 7960, shown in Figure 6.7, can also automatically detect the type of paper that's loaded.

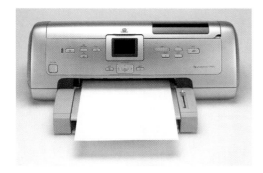

Figure 6.7
HP Photosmart 7960

Duplex printing capabilities Duplex printing is another feature available only on the latest ink-jet printers. Duplex printing is two-sided printing. The printer automatically reroutes the printed page to properly format and print the second side. Although you wouldn't use duplex printing for traditional scrapbooking, it can be a wonderful feature for doing craft projects, printing note cards and brag books, and printing calendars. Some manufacturers offer it as an option. The PIXMA series of printers from Canon, such as the PIXMA iP4000 (shown in Figure 6.8), automatically include duplex printing.

Figure 6.8
The Canon PIXMA iP4000 not only connects your digital camera, but it also offers two-sided printing.

Canon also offers a "brag book in a box," which is a photo album kit with paper and a special easy-to-use album. You print your photos on both sides of the double-sided photo paper, gently spread the cover of the album, and then slip in the pages. The album holds the pages with a light spring action until you choose to change the photos in the brag book.

Scrapbooking doesn't have one perfect printer. You can find many models with a variety of features at all prices. The single-most important feature is still the quality of the print. Choose a printer first by the color, tonal range, and detail of a sample photo and second by the added features you'd use.

Note: You may come across the terms *PostScript* and *RIP*. Both relate to printing mathematically described shapes (or *vectors*) rather than pixels. Adobe Photoshop Elements automatically "flattens" or "simplifies" any vector, such as text or a shape, into pixels before printing. With Adobe Photoshop Elements you don't need a PostScript printer to print photos and scrapbook pages.

Shopping List for Ink-Jet Printers

The following is a shopping list for buying an ink-jet printer:

- ☑ **Print size:** Choose a printer capable of at least letter-sized prints.
- ☑ **Resolution:** You'll want 1440 dpi minimum.
- ☑ **Droplet size:** Get the smallest possible droplet size and the most colors available. You'll want 4-picoliter or smaller droplet size with at least six colors of ink, or 2-picoliter or smaller droplet size with at least four colors of ink.
- ☑ **Ink:** Use pigment ink for the greatest longevity of prints. Use dye ink for the largest range of colors.
- ☑ **Cartridges:** Get individual color ink cartridges if possible.
- ☑ **Bonus features:** Check for the following optional features:

  Built-in memory card slots

  Multiple paper feed paths

  CD/DVD media printing

  Duplex printing
- ☑ **Cable:** Get a quality USB cable no longer than 6 feet, or 2 meters.

The Care and Feeding of Your Ink-Jet Printer

The following are some guidelines to follow for getting the most out of your printer regardless of the brand or model:

Install the right driver   To be able to print from your computer, you need to install a *driver*. When you first get a printer, you'll find a CD with software applications and the printer drivers for various operating systems, such as Windows XP, or Mac OS X. Since manufacturers are constantly updating the drivers, it's best to go to your printer manufacturer's website and see which driver you need (see Figure 6.9). Installing the driver also installs information about the specific papers from the manufacturer, telling the printer how to spray the dots of ink on those papers.

Tip: If you update your computer operating system, you'll need to update the printer driver. Always check the manufacturer's website for appropriate drivers.

Run print head alignment   Before using a printer for the first time, and anytime you move the printer, run a print head alignment. This sounds complicated; however, you do nothing more than put a few sheets of paper into the paper feed of the printer and select the alignment in the printer driver software. The printer takes care of the rest. (Figure 6.10).

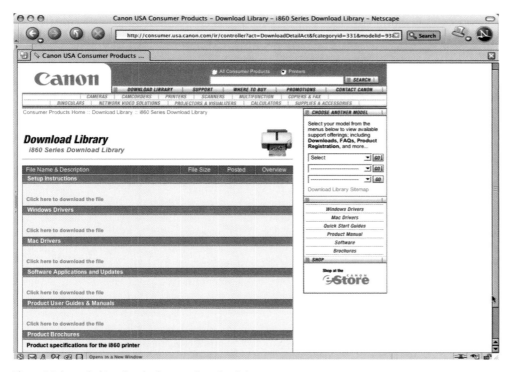

Figure 6.9 A sample driver download page on Canon's website

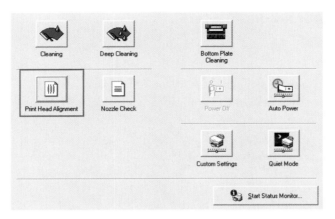

Figure 6.10 A sample print head alignment dialog box

Find the right printer cable A poor-quality or overly long cable can cause a bad connection resulting in data errors or miss-prints. The printer may work for a while and then suddenly not be recognized by the computer.

Purchase a good-quality, shielded cable from a known manufacturer, such as Belkin. The guidelines for printer cable lengths vary, but a short cable is generally best.

Use the on/off button Always use the on/off button on the printer. This is especially important if you plug the power cable of the printer into an extension strip, surge protector, or a battery backup power supply called a UPS (which stands for *uninterruptible power supply*). The printer has a special startup and shutdown routine it needs to go through—charging the heads when it starts and parking the carriage and sealing the printer head area when it shuts down. Flipping the switch on an external power source stops the printer from going through these steps. A sudden printer shut down can cause the ink to spray inside the printer, ruin the next pieces of paper you use, and even damage the printer. Some people choose to leave the printer on all the time to save the minuscule amount of ink that's wasted in the startup process. However, if you have a power outage, your printer will not shut down properly, causing a lot more problems. As a general rule, leave the printer plugged into a powered UPS or surge protector and turn the printer off using the printer's power button.

 Note: Always use the printer's power button to turn the printer on and off.

Keep dust away If possible, cover the ink-jet printer when it isn't in use. Keeping dust out of the printer helps avoid clogged ink-jets and other problems. Dust will stick to ink wherever it finds it. If you leave paper in a top paper feed, the top sheet can accumulate dust, which will be drawn into the printer when you print that sheet. When loading sheets of paper into an ink-jet printer, always fan the papers to remove the minute particles left over from the original cutting and packaging. This is especially true of specialty and art papers.

Check your ink levels   Check the *ink levels* on a regular basis so you don't run out of ink in the middle of a print job. You'll usually find an option to check your cartridges in the printer software. If one of the ink levels looks low, you can have a replacement cartridge ready to replace it. As a general rule, leave the ink cartridges in their slots inside the printer even if you aren't using the printer. Without the cartridges in place, the ink-jet heads can dry out or get clogged with leftover ink or dust particles.

Run a nozzle check and ink-jet head cleaning   If your prints show lines or missed spots, you can run a *nozzle check* to see if an ink-jet head is clogged (Figure 6.11). It's also a good idea to run a nozzle check after you haven't used the printer for a period of time. Put a letter-sized piece of plain paper in the printer, and select nozzle check in the printer driver software. The printer will print a test pattern. If all the nozzles are firing, the pattern will be complete. If you see gaps, the printer may have a clog along a supply line or on one of the ink-jet heads. You'll need to select the maintenance button for an ink-jet head cleaning. The printer runs a cleaning cycle and charges the heads. When it has finished, you run another nozzle check to see if the pattern prints clearly. You may need to repeat the cleaning cycle and nozzle check one or two times until the test pattern prints completely without gaps. This process uses some ink, but the printer will regain its full capabilities. If the nozzle check pattern still prints incompletely after two or three cleaning cycles, turn off the printer using the power button on the printer. Let the printer sit for 4–24 hours. Then turn it on and try printing the nozzle check pattern again. The pattern should print clearly. The ink that was sent through the printer head during the cleaning will work through the clogged areas while the printer is off and the carriage is in the parked position.

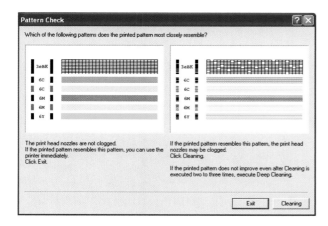

Figure 6.11
Sample nozzle check and head cleaning dialog box

Choosing the Right Ink and Paper

Today's photo ink-jet printers are so good that you can tell when a print isn't a traditional film-processed photograph only by looking through a 10-power magnifying glass or loupe. However, this quality depends upon a complex system in which the printer sprays out one type of ink in a specific pattern, optimized for a specific paper. The printer, ink, and paper are all engineered to work together.

The life of your prints and the life of your printer also depend on the type of inks and papers you use. Always make sure you check the specifications of the printer model, and choose the inks and papers accordingly.

Printing with Photo Services

Printing your digital photos on your own printer is definitely convenient. It can also be costly and time-consuming, especially when you have a large number of photographs to print. You can still take advantage of digital technology for craft and scrapbook projects without printing all your photos yourself. Take digital photos, scan old photographs, negatives, and slides, and then use Adobe Photoshop Elements to repair and enhance the images. But when you need standard-sized prints and many of them, you can upload the image files or send them on CD media to an online photo service such as PhotoWorks .com (Figure 6.12), Adobe Photoshop Services, Nikonnet.com, and others. The prints are mailed back to you, along with any media you sent. Other services, such as Ritzpix .com and Costco, let you pick up your photos in a few hours. Most of these services and companies offer true photographic prints, printed with professional digital photographic printers on light-sensitive photo papers.

Figure 6.12
PhotoWorks upload page

Even including the cost of shipping, using an online photo service can be an easy and affordable way of getting all the prints you need for your scrapbooks, with duplicates for family and friends.

The tendency with digital cameras is to take many more photos than you'd ever want to print. Still, you don't know if someone else would prefer one shot over another. With an online photo service, you can upload all the photo files that may be good, creating an online "album." You can then send e-mail invitations to your friends and family to look at the photo albums online. And they can order their favorites in the sizes they want. Such services can also put your photos on CD, print complete photo albums and brag books, and help you make DVD and VHS videos using your still photographs.

One Last Thought...

Use the best of both worlds. Make your snapshots the best they can be using Adobe Photoshop Elements and your computer. Then upload these and order standard-sized photo prints and all the duplicates from an online photo service or other photo printing service. Use a photo ink-jet printer to make instant photos, to make quick brag books, and to print all the elements for your pages and projects. A photo ink-jet printer is also perfect for printing special cards, large- and different-sized photographs, and all the designs you can imagine using the special effects in Adobe Photoshop Elements.

More Tools for Scrapbooking and Archiving

Computer hardware and software are simply additional scrapbooking tools like scissors and glue. Hardware is the stuff you can touch, and software is the invisible magic that controls the hardware. Peripheral hardware *includes any computer hardware that isn't inside the computer box itself. Certain peripherals are essential to digital scrapbooking, both for the added creative possibilities and for helping to safeguard your memories. We'll briefly describe the most important items in this chapter.*

7

Chapter Contents

Pen tablet, the mighty unmouse
Monitors matter
Preserving your images
Archiving digital files

Pen Tablet, the Mighty Unmouse

Even when you type with a computer, you need a mouse to access a variety of tools and menus. Using a *pen tablet* instead of a mouse offers more control and creative possibilities for all your digital artwork and photography. And for digital scrapbooking, a pen tablet is an indispensable tool. A pen tablet, also called a *digitizing tablet*, or *graphics tablet*, is a flat, electronic pad you use with a *stylus*, or electronic pen. Hover over the *active area* in the center of the tablet to move the cursor across the screen, and touch the active area with the stylus to select a menu item or click. Since you can hold the stylus lightly and move your hand and arm rather than just your wrist, a pen tablet is more comfortable and ergonomic than a computer mouse (see Figure 7.1). And you can use the stylus to trace images or draw freehand in many graphics applications. Professional artists, designers, and photographers generally use Wacom pen tablets, the best-known and most responsive graphics tablets on the market.

Figure 7.1
Graphire3 tablet in use

Getting Comfortable

Once you have a pen tablet, you may find that it's better for all your computer work. The stylus for a Wacom tablet has no batteries or cord, and looks and feels like a real pen. Wacom tablets also come with a special battery-free and cordless mouse. The Wacom mouse is ergonomically designed and includes buttons for clicking and a finger wheel for scrolling. You can use the stylus and cordless mouse alternately to minimize strain and maximize comfort depending on the task. For example, when reading documents, use the tablet's mouse to click or scroll up and down pages. Then switch to the stylus to draw with a graphics application or to select objects or text.

Taking Control

In addition to being more comfortable to use, a pen tablet gives you more control than any traditional computer mouse. The tablet technology responds more quickly and accurately. You can use the stylus to select areas on your photos or artwork with pinpoint precision, and without accidentally moving or changing areas you want to preserve. When you place the stylus on the left of the tablet, the cursor is at the left on the screen, and so on. Wacom calls this *absolute positioning*. No more scooting the mouse around like a toy car (see Figure 7.2).

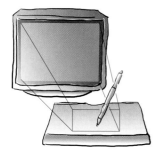

Figure 7.2
Absolute positioning
the monitor screen corresponds to
the active area of the tablet.

A stylus pen also gives you *pressure-sensitive* control, so the stylus responds to your drawing style: the harder you press, the more you affect your drawing or your photo; conversely, the lighter your touch, the less color or the thinner the line you'll apply.

More than 100 leading software applications are specifically designed for use with a stylus pen, many with tools that work only when you connect a pen tablet to the computer. For example, Adobe Photoshop Elements has at least 15 customizable tools that are controlled with pen pressure. The Wacom stylus pen even has a pressure-sensitive eraser on one end, just like a traditional pencil. Flip the stylus pen over, and you can erase text, pencil, pen marks, and even oil and watercolor paints. In Figure 7.3, the box on the left shows lines and brush strokes done with a high-quality traditional mouse in Photoshop Elements. The box on the right shows what you can do with the same tools using a Wacom stylus.

14-pixel hard-edge brush   14-pixel hard-edge brush

26-pixel soft-edge brush   26-pixel soft-edge brush

75-pixel hard-edge brush   75-pixel hard-edge brush

Figure 7.3
Brush strokes in Adobe Photoshop Elements applied with a mouse (left). Brush strokes in Adobe Photoshop Elements applied with a Wacom stylus and tablet (right).

Choosing and Using a Pen Tablet

Wacom makes a number of different pen tablet models (see Figure 7.4 and Figure 7.5). The *Graphire* tablets are more affordable, but the *Intuos* tablets are more sensitive and offer more features. Both come in various sizes. The size always refers to the *active area*, not to the overall dimensions of the tablet itself.

Figure 7.4 Wacom Graphire3 pen tablets in both sizes   **Figure 7.5** Wacom Intuos3 pen tablets

You use a stylus pen in the same way you use a mouse: by focusing on the monitor and not your hand. Moving the stylus just above the tablet is the same as scooting the mouse. Touching the stylus down is the same as clicking a mouse. You should focus on the tablet only when tracing something. Place a photograph or a drawing on the active area and you can trace it with the stylus using various graphics applications.

Setting Pen Tablet Properties or Preferences

Wacom pen tablets allow you to customize the stylus and the special mouse using the pen tablet properties or preferences. You can choose the amount of pressure needed to erase, click, and draw with the stylus, and you can program the *DuoSwitch* buttons on the stylus and the many buttons on the tablet mouse. Set these buttons to Open, Close, or any frequently used keystrokes. Or set one side of the DuoSwitch or one mouse button to Pop-up Menu, and set this menu to display your most often used actions or keys, so you can use your tablet on your lap and completely avoid reaching for your keyboard. Figure 7.6 shows an example of pop-up menu settings for opening, closing, selecting, and more.

The best way to learn to use a graphics tablet is to set up the tablet properties or preferences. Then open a blank document in a graphics application, such as Photoshop Elements, which is included free with Wacom tablets. Draw and paint, then erase, or delete the entire page without any dust or paint to clean up. Talk about artistic freedom!

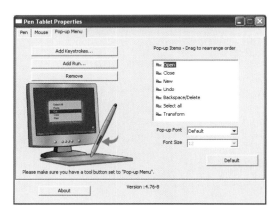

Figure 7.6
Pop-up menu choices

Monitors Matter

The monitor is your window to your images. If your window is dull, is distorted, or changes colors, it will affect all your work. Have you ever gone into a large appliance store and looked at all the televisions tuned to the same channel yet all showing different colors? If they were *calibrated*, or set to one color standard, it would be much easier to compare them. A monitor *profile* is a description of how the monitor displays color at one particular moment. Calibrating and profiling a computer monitor so that it shows consistent, predictable color is most important for creative work and easier on the eyes for general computing.

Although you can adjust the monitor with the control knobs and set the colors to please your eyes, how can you know if your settings show the actual colors in the image file? The printer gets all the attention if the colors you print aren't what you see on the screen. But it may be your monitor's fault.

Various "eyeball" methods exist to calibrate and profile a computer monitor. Adobe Gamma is automatically loaded into the Control Panel on a Windows system when you install Photoshop Elements. The Display Calibrator Assistant is built into the System Preferences on a Mac. When using any "eyeball" method, set the monitor control knobs to the middle position, dim the lights in the room, and wear neutral colors, such as gray or black, so that your clothing doesn't reflect from the screen and alter your color vision.

Using a *colorimeter* to calibrate and profile a monitor is easier and results in more consistent color. A colorimeter is a small device that measures color. The Eye-One Display from GretagMacbeth or the Optix from Monaco are affordable and accurate tools to calibrate and profile any monitor. And unlike other computer equipment, a calibrator is an investment that can be used on all monitors, sometimes extending the life of an old monitor. The appendix in this book shows step-by-step instructions for using the Eye-One Display colorimeter and profiling software.

What to Look for in a Monitor

Monitor specifications are filled with acronyms and numbers. This section provides some basic definitions and shopping list recommendations for choosing a monitor for scrapbooking or any computer work.

Two basic types of computer monitors exist: CRTs and LCDs. A CRT (*cathode ray tube*) is more like a traditional TV set. A CRT has a hard glass face, takes up a lot of room on your desk, and uses more electrical power. An LCD (*liquid crystal display*) has liquid crystals sandwiched between other layers in the viewing area. An LCD, also called a *flat-panel display*, uses much less desktop space and less electricity. LCDs aren't the same as *flat-screen* monitors, which are flat-screen CRTs.

Refresh rate on a CRT refers to how many times per second the screen refreshes even when the image isn't changing. The flicker is there whether or not you see it. The higher the *refresh rate*, the more stable the image will appear and the less strain on your eyes. LCDs have no refresh rate since they use different components. It's easier to stare at an LCD for long periods of time.

Viewable image size is the diagonal measurement of the displayed image regardless of the advertised size of the monitor. CRTs usually require a margin around the image, but LCDs fill the image to the edges, so a 17-inch CRT may have the same viewable image size as a 15-inch LCD.

Contrast ratio defines the range of shades the monitor can display. The higher the number, the smoother the gradations of tone and color, and the better your images will look.

Resolution for monitors refers to the maximum number of *pixels*, or little squares of light, both horizontal and vertical, that can display on the screen at one time. The bigger the numbers, the smaller the images may appear, but the more items you can see on the screen at once.

Dot pitch (CRT) or *pixel pitch* (LCD) is a measurement for overall sharpness and quality. The smaller the number, the crisper the image will be on your screen.

Sixteen million colors is a standard to see the full range of colors in your photographs.

A *video card* inside the computer controls both types of monitors. Check the requirements of the monitor and the connectors. Video cards may have Analog (VGA) or digital (DVI) connectors. Adapters exist to match the monitor cable if necessary.

Shopping List for Monitors

☑ **Refresh rate (CRT only):** Get 85 hertz (Hz) or more. A higher number is better.

☑ **Viewable image size:** The bigger, the better.

☑ **Contrast ratio:** Get 300:1 or higher. A higher number is better.

☑ **Resolution:** Make sure to get 1024×768 pixels or larger.

☑ **Dot pitch (CRT) and pixel pitch (LCD):** You'll want 0.26–0.29 millimeters (mm) or smaller. Smaller numbers are better.

☑ **Colors:** You'll want 16 million colors.

☑ **Video card and connectors:** Make sure the monitor requirements and connectors match.

Preserving Your Images

One of the biggest advantages of using a computer for scrapbooking and photography is the many archiving possibilities. Digital information should last forever. However, how you save the data, the media you save it on, and where you store the media all make a difference in the preservation of digital files. Having both paper memory albums and digital archives is the best way to preserve your memories.

Making Prints That Last

With today's ink-jet printers, you can produce images that look just as good or better than a traditional photograph. But will that print last as long? According to Wilhelm Imaging Research (www.wilhelm-research.com) and the Rochester Institute of Technology (www.rit.edu/ipi), some digital prints are expected to resist fading longer than traditional photographic prints. Both Wilhelm and RIT conduct accelerated-age testing for photographic print permanence. Specific ink and paper combinations are the determining factors in the longevity of a print. The same is true of photographs printed with the traditional processing, called *silver halide*. Fine-art black-and-white prints from 50 or more years ago were also produced with specific techniques and quality papers. Generally, color photographs from traditional photo labs are expected to last anywhere from 20 to 60 years, depending on the chemicals and papers used and the method of storage.

Note: With the digital technology in newer scanners and software, it's possible to restore some older faded photographs. Do it now so you can archive them digitally.

Most longevity testing is done for prints in *display conditions*, meaning framed under glass and displayed on a wall with indoor lighting. *How* photographs or any artwork, including paintings and pastels, are stored and *where* they're stored make a big

difference in their preservation. Different types and
amounts of light, as well as moisture and air con-
taminants, can attack prints and art, as well as the
paper or canvas itself, which is why museums take
such great care with their displays.

Using the Right Ink

If you print photos and scrapbook pages to keep as heirlooms, you want those prints to
last at least as long as the manufacturer's claims. Each ink-jet printer is designed to
spray ink droplets in a specific fashion, depending on the viscosity as well as the color
balance of the inks. And since any dust or dirt in an ink cartridge can clog an ink-jet nozzle, ruining the prints and possibly the printer, many manufacturers fill their cartridges in
"clean rooms." An inexpensive replacement cartridge may have a greater chance of
being contaminated. It's always safest to use only the manufacturers' ink cartridges,
especially during your printer's warranty period. Using other ink brands usually invali-
dates the warranty.

Some specialty ink companies do have their inks tested for quality and fade
resistance by the same independent testing facilities as the printer manufacturers. Lyson
has been making and testing ink-jet inks for more than ten years and may be a good
choice for an older printer. Check the Lyson.com website for prices and test results.

Two basic types of ink-jet ink are available today for desktop printers: *dye* and
pigment. Each is specific to the printer model and has different characteristics. Dyes
sink into the paper fibers like the dye you may use on a piece of cloth. Dye ink prints
have the widest *color gamut*, or color range, but are more prone to fading. Pigments
are colors in powder form, similar to the colors in oil and watercolor paints. The pigments are blended with an emulsion so they can spray from an ink-jet nozzle and combine with the paper surface. Pigment ink prints generally have a smaller color range,
can be used only with certain papers, and are more prone to scratches. However, pigment ink prints will usually last longer than prints with dye inks. When choosing an
ink-jet printer, get print samples using both types of ink on various papers. Both dye
and pigment ink-jet prints kept in a properly stored scrapbook should outlast the print
permanence ratings for the same prints in display conditions.

Using the Right Paper

You can't use just any acid-free paper and expect to get long-lasting or quality prints.
All ink-jet papers are coated to match the spray patterns designed by the printer manufacturer. Even when you're printing journaling segments, you should use ink-jet paper
to get clear, long-lasting prints. However, not all ink-jet papers are acid-free, and papers
with optical brighteners can reduce the life of an ink-jet print. Always check the specifications on the paper package.

Certain glossy photo-type ink-jet papers are optimized to produce long-lasting
prints. For example, a black-and-white photo printed using the HP photo dye inks and
HP Premium Plus Photo Paper received a permanence rating from Wilhelm of 115
years in display conditions. A color print using the same type of HP ink and paper
resulted in fade resistance for up to 73 years. Color prints using either Epson Pigment

or Epson Dye inks on Epson's Ultra Smooth Fine Art paper produced some of the longest-lasting prints for matte paper surfaces.

Other manufacturers make papers producing long-lasting, high-quality ink-jet prints. Using different papers doesn't invalidate the printer's warranty. Red River Papers (www.redriverpaper.com) and Moab Papers (www.moabpaper.com) both make excellent photographic and fine-art ink-jet papers in various sizes and surfaces, from glossy to matte. They include double-sided papers, pre-scored greeting cards with matching envelopes, and scrapbook-sized album pages. Check their websites to see which ink-jet printers and printer settings are best suited to their papers, as well as the expected life of the prints. Lineco (www.lineco.com) produces a line of PopArt album kits, including album covers; acid-free, lignin-free pages for ink-jet printers; interleaving sheets; and a storage box.

Archiving Digital Files

Whether you print your own or send them out to be printed, once your photos are digital, you have a file that's easier to store and easier to find than those negative strips you have stored…somewhere. Your files are usually saved to the hard drive inside your computer. Since image files are large, they can quickly fill up an internal drive. Further, everyone who uses that computer can access, change, or accidentally delete them. Fortunately, you have other, safer choices for storing digital archives.

Files from a digital camera may be in various formats, including the camera's proprietary RAW format, TIFF (.tif), or JPEG (.jpg). Get into the habit of copying these directly to a CD without changing them so you'll always have a copy of the originals intact. Photoshop Elements can open many types of files, converting them to the Photoshop (.psd) format when you work on the images. To save image files for storage, it's best to save them as TIFF (.tif) files, the most widely accessible file format used today. Small JPEG files are good for e-mailing; however, each time you open, change, and then save a JPEG file again, it loses some data. TIFF files are larger, but they preserve all the data and can save the layers you create in Photoshop Elements. By staying aware of the technology changes, you can always convert your files if another format becomes predominant in the future.

Digital Storage Options

Always make duplicates of the files and store them in different ways and in separate places. You have some choices for both temporary and more permanent digital storage.

USB Flash Drives

USB flash drives such as the Lexar's Jump drives or SanDisk's Cruzer drives are convenient temporary storage systems (see Figure 7.7). These are small, solid-state memory drives you can plug into the USB port of your computer to copy files. Flash drives are perfect for moving files from one computer to another without a network. Today, USB flash drives come in all sizes from 32 megabytes (MB) to 2 gigabytes (GB).

External Hard Drives

In addition to CD and DVD media, external hard drives are the best temporary and permanent storage for digital scrapbooking files. The large capacity drives from Maxtor, for example, can store from 80 to 300 gigabytes (GB), or years of photos and scrapbook pages. Your computer's internal hard drive may be much smaller and has to store the operating system, applications, and other files. External drives are economical for storage, in terms of cost per megabyte, as well as practical. And if you change computers, the external drive and all your projects move with you (see Figure 7.8).

Figure 7.7 The SanDisk Cruzer USB flash drive

Figure 7.8 The Maxtor OneTouch provides large storage and automatic backup for the entire system.

An external hard drive is a necessity if you share your computer with other members of your household. Would you leave all your scrapbooking supplies, partially finished pages, and photographs on the kitchen table when the family comes in for dinner? By saving all your photos and scrapbook pages on an external hard drive, you can simply disconnect that drive when someone else uses the computer. When you're ready to scrap, plug in the external drive and your projects are just as you left them. Plus, if you use the scanners and printers at scrapbook stores or a friend's house, your external drive is perfect for transporting large files from one computer to another. Ideally, you could store one external hard drive filled with your heritage photos in a safety deposit box and use another external hard drive to create more projects.

Here are some key guidelines for using external hard drives:

- Don't move or bump a drive when it's plugged in and working.
- Select a high-quality hard drive, such as the Maxtor One Touch or Maxtor Personal.
- Always use a *UPS*, an *uninterruptible power supply*. See "Saving Your Equipment with a UPS" later in this chapter.

CD and DVD Archiving

Copying your photo files and scrapbook pages on a CD or DVD is an inexpensive and convenient storage method. CDs and DVDs are optical, not magnetic media. They aren't affected by airport X-rays or magnetic detectors. CD and DVD readers and writers access the data or "burn" the data to the disc using a laser light. CD/DVD is the most common form of digital data storage today.

You must also take precautions with CD and DVD media. They're subject to corrosion from many sources, including ozone, ultraviolet light, chemicals, high temperatures, humidity, and static electricity. In addition, technology changes quickly. Remember the floppy disk? The drives that read CD and DVD today may be obsolete in the future.

Here are some key guidelines for digital archiving on CD and DVD media:

- Burn two copies, date them for references, and keep them in separate locations.
- Use CD (CD-R) and DVD write-once (DVD+R) or (DVD-R) media for archiving your files. Rewritable discs aren't as reliable for long-term storage.

- Use name-brand CDs and DVDs. Don't buy the least expensive ones available.
- If another type of media becomes predominant at some point in the future, transfer the information to the new media.

Guidelines for Storing CDs and DVDs

We compiled the following information with permission from a report by Fred Byers of the National Institute of Standards and Technology (http://www.itl.nist.gov/div895/carefordisc).

- Don't touch the recording surface. Handle the discs by the outer edge or the center hole.
- Don't scratch or bend CDs and DVDs.
- Label only using non-solvent-based, soft felt-tipped permanent markers.

  If possible, write only in the clear inner hub or mirror band on the CD.

  Never use adhesive labels.

  Never write on the data side.

  You can use ink-jet *printable* CD and DVD discs.
- Clean the discs before recording, before playing, and before storing.

  Use a bulb blower to blow off dust.

  Wipe with a clean cotton fabric in a straight line from the center of the disc toward the outer edge.

  Don't wipe in a circular motion.

  Use isopropyl alcohol (rubbing alcohol) or methanol to remove stubborn dirt.
- Store discs in their individual cases in a clean, cool, dry, and dark environment.

  Store discs in the cases vertically, like books on a shelf.

  Remove paper labels from the inside of the cases.

  Return discs to storage cases immediately after use.

  Open a new CD/DVD package only when you're ready to burn a disc.

  Don't stock pile discs or purchase too many in advance.

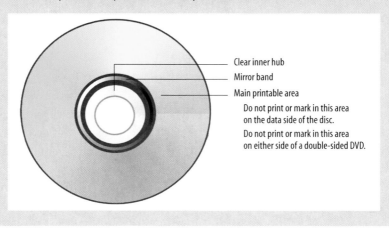

Clear inner hub
Mirror band
Main printable area
Do not print or mark in this area on the data side of the disc.
Do not print or mark in this area on either side of a double-sided DVD.

Saving Your Equipment with a UPS

Wherever you live, the power that comes into your house isn't constant or "clean." *Brownouts*, short-term decreases in voltage levels, and *overvoltages*, power surges and spikes, happen all day long. These may be imperceptible, but they change the voltage going to your equipment and can eventually cause damage or corrupt files. *Surge protectors* can prevent surges from reaching your equipment. (see Figure 7.9).

Blackouts are sudden and complete losses of utility power. If your computer is on, a blackout may cause data loss and hard drive damage. A *UPS*, uninterruptible power supply, can protect your computer, monitor, external hard drive, modem, and even an ink-jet printer. Since scanners and laser printers draw a lot of power, use a separate UPS or use a surge protector for these items. A UPS works differently than a surge protector. It offers surge protection and also includes a battery to keep the power at a constant level. Instead of suddenly losing power during a blackout, the UPS keeps your computer and other equipment running and alerts you to save your work and shut down properly. A UPS can save your whole system. It's essential for protecting the internal hard drive in your computer and an external one, plus all the files on those drives. Reliable UPS models such as the Belkin UPS in Figure 7.10 even include a warranty for recovering data if your hard drive were to malfunction because of a failure of the UPS battery backup.

Figure 7.9
A Belkin surge protector

Figure 7.10
This UPS from Belkin offers surge protection, battery backup, voltage regulation, and a data recovery warranty.

Here are some key guidelines for your UPS:

- Always plug the UPS directly into the wall receptacle.
- Don't plug a surge protector into a UPS or the UPS into a surge protector.
- Choose a UPS with enough power for multiple devices.
- Don't plug a laser printer or a scanner into the same UPS as your computer.

One Last Thought...

Scrapbooking is all about memory and photo preservation. We want the future generations to see and feel what we did. We want our grandchildren to see what their parents were like as children. Photographs are the best records of the past, and archiving is all about keeping that record intact. A computer and peripheral hardware can greatly increase the artistic possibilities while preserving those memories more safely than using only traditional paper, scissors, and glue. You want a tangible archive—a paper-and-ink copy that will last. And you need a digital backup. With your photos and scrapbooks in both printed and digital form, your archived memories can last long into the future.

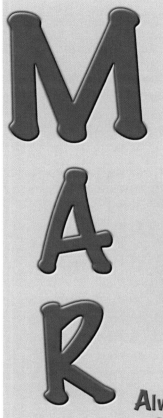

M
A
R
C

From Superman

To James Bond

Always a
Superhero

Getting Started with Photoshop Elements

Using a computer and Photoshop Elements opens up so many new ways to create scrapbook pages. Not only can you improve your photos, making them better than they were, but you can include old photographs and never alter the originals. Elements offers organizational methods for scrapbooking and for archival storage. And changing the size of your images without paying film-processing charges at a photo lab is economical—and fun. Using a computer as a scrapbooking tool can preserve your memories and unleash your creativity.

8

Chapter Contents

Why use Photoshop Elements?
Before you start, have a backup
Organizing your files with Photoshop Elements
Photoshop Elements editing tools and palettes

Why Use Photoshop Elements?

Although it wasn't created specifically for scrapbookers, Adobe Photoshop Elements is the most comprehensive application for scrapbooking available. Other "scrapbooking software" programs offer basic color corrections, page designs, or help for scanning 12×12 pages. You may even get such applications free when purchasing hardware or other supplies. Unfortunately, these simplified or single-purpose applications don't offer all the functions that scrapbookers need for creating memorable photos or pages.

Photoshop Elements is intended for photographers. It has many of the same features as Adobe Photoshop CS, and it even has some that Photoshop doesn't include. Yet Elements is much easier to use.

With Photoshop Elements 3, you can scan images, fix red-eye, size and crop photos, make color corrections, repair old photos, and turn color photos into black-and-white or sepia-toned images. For scrapbookers, Elements can help you create page backgrounds, design page toppers and tags, stylize type, make photo frames, create the entire scrapbook page at any size, and even scan a 12×12-inch page with a letter-sized scanner.

Note: Image-editing applications are RAM hungry. Photoshop Elements requires at least 256MB of RAM. In addition to the operating system itself, every program that's open uses memory. To get the most out of a limited amount of RAM, close all your other applications when you work in Photoshop Elements.

Before You Start, Have a Backup

Digital archiving is one of the major advantages of scrapbooking with your computer. Whether you start by scanning traditional photos or use a digital camera, the first step is to get a backup CD of the original files. Then make a *contact sheet*, a small photo index of every image on the CD, as a visual list to help you find the images easily.

Obtain or Burn a CD

You don't need a digital camera and printer to use digital photos. If you use a film camera, you can take or send the film to a photo lab or online photo service to convert your film photos to digital media and get a CD with your photos on them. Mail-order photo services such as Adobe Photoshop Services and PhotoWorks.com offer photo CDs and a variety of print sizes. The prints and CDs are conveniently mailed to you. And with your digital files and photo albums now stored on the company's website, you have an additional form of temporary storage.

If you have a digital camera, copy all your photos to a new folder on your computer and use a CD burner to make a CD with all the originals unaltered. Don't open the images—they're originals, like "digital negatives." If you scan old prints, negatives, slides, or any documents, save the scanned files to a folder and "burn" a CD of the original scans before you use them in your projects. If you make a change or inadvertently delete the file as you're working, you won't have to rescan the image.

> **Note:** Whether you use a scanned image or a digital camera photograph, always work on a copy of the original, and keep the original on a stored CD.

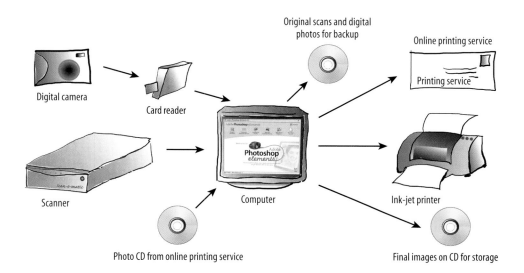

Create a Contact Sheet

A printed contact sheet will make finding a specific photo much easier. Launch Photoshop Elements 3, and follow the steps in the next sections depending on your operating system.

Creating a Contact Sheet in Windows

In Windows, you'll see a welcome screen.

1. Select View and Organize Photos. This starts the Organizer.
2. Click the Camera icon, and choose From Files and Folders (see Figure 8.1).
3. Navigate to the folder with your digital photos or to the photo CD.
4. Select the folder or CD by clicking it once, and choose Get Photos (see Figure 8.2). Your photos are imported into the Organizer's main window (see Figure 8.3). The dialog box reminds you that the only photos in the main window are those that were just imported. Click OK to continue.

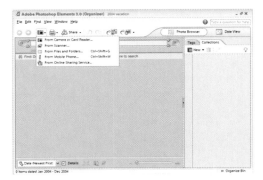

Figure 8.1 Choosing the files and folders to bring into the Organizer

Figure 8.2 Get Photos from Files and Folders dialog box

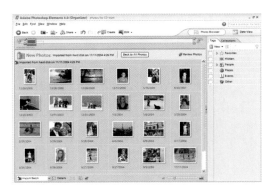

Figure 8.3

Photoshop Elements Organizer with photo thumbnails

5. Go to File > Print. A dialog box will ask if you want to print all the currently displayed photos. Click OK to continue.

6. In the Print Photos dialog box shown in Figure 8.4, select the name of your printer. Click the box next to the printer name to show the printer preferences.

Figure 8.4

Print Selected Photos dialog box

7. Choose the media type and other printer specific settings.

8. Click the Page Setup tab and choose Custom (or User Defined) for the Page Size. Set the width and height each at 4.75 inches, for a standard CD jewel case. Click OK until you're back in the Print Photos dialog box.

9. Select Contact Sheet for the type of print, 5 columns for the layout, and check the Filename box for the text label.

10. Click Print to print the contact sheet(s) for your image CD.

Creating a Contact Sheet on a Macintosh

If you're using a Mac, close the Photoshop Elements 3 welcome screen. Elements opens in the Editor mode.

1. Click Standard Edit at the top right of the screen.
2. Select File > Contact Sheet II.
3. In the Contact Sheet II dialog box, shown in Figure 8.5, click Choose and then navigate to the folder or CD with your new images.

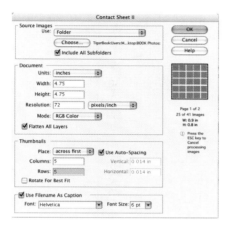

Figure 8.5

Contact Sheet II dialog box for setting up your contact sheet preferences

4. Set the Document Width and Height both to 4.75 inches, the standard size for a CD jewel case. A resolution of 72 pixels/inch is fine for tiny thumbnails.
5. Choose RGB Color for the mode, and leave Flatten All Layers checked.
6. Choose the number of columns and rows you want for your thumbnails; 5 is a good setting for both.
7. Choose a font and font size for the thumbnail captions. Use a font such as Helvetica and a small font size such as 6 so the filename will be completely printed.
8. Click OK, and Photoshop Elements will build a contact sheet.
9. Go to File > Print to print the contact sheet.

Organizing Your Files with Photoshop Elements

Once your files are in digital format and you have a backup CD and contact sheet of the original photos or scans, it's time to start digital scrapbooking. Just as with traditional scrapbooking, you may want to organize your photos for your pages. Using Photoshop Elements, you can prepare folders and group all the elements for a scrapbook page. Photoshop Elements 3 includes a new Organizer workspace for Windows users, which has similar functions to the ones in iPhoto on the Mac.

Organizer Workspace (Windows Only)

The Organizer offers many tools to organize your files. From the Organizer, you can print a contact sheet as we just explained, reorganize the images into virtual photo albums called *collections*, view the images by date on a calendar, or assign keyword tags to photos so you can categorize and find all the similarly tagged images at one time.

In Windows, start Elements in the Organizer workspace by choosing View and Organize Photos from the Welcome menu. Click the camera icon, and Elements collects images from cameras, card readers, scanners, or file folders already on your computer and automatically arranges them by date.

Describing all the organizational possibilities in Photoshop Elements 3 is beyond the scope of this book. However, two special features are so exciting for anyone reviewing photos for a scrapbook or other album, we need to mention them.

You'll find both *Photo Compare* and *Photo Review* under View in the Organizer menu bar. You often need to decide between two or more similar photos for a scrapbook. *Photo Compare* offers a large, side-by-side preview of your photos.

To compare photos, follow these steps:

1. Select two or more photos by Ctrl+clicking their thumbnails.

2. Go to View > Photo Compare. A new window opens with just the selected photos (see Figure 8.6).

Figure 8.6
A side-by-side comparison helps you choose which photos to place in your scrapbook.

The *Photo Review* feature turns sorting through all your photos into an emotional experience.

To review photos, follow these steps:

1. Select as many photos as you want to review by Ctrl+clicking their thumbnails, or select the entire group by clicking the film roll icon above the group of photos.

2. Go to View > Photo Review.

3. In the Photo Review dialog box, choose the background music and any other viewing options, and click OK. A new window opens with a full-screen preview of the first photo. Click the Start button (a white triangle in a green circle in the top control bar), sit back, and enjoy a slide show of your memories.

iPhoto (Mac Only)

Mac users can use iPhoto to access many similar functions of Photoshop Elements' Organizer. Launch iPhoto which is included with Mac OS X. Select File > Import and import the photos from a folder or photo CD and choose the slide show or any of the other organizational tools. See Figure 8.7.

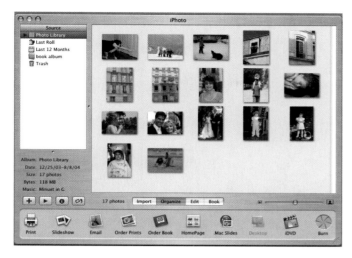

Figure 8.7
Organizing with Apple's
iPhoto on the Mac

Editor Workspace

In both Windows and on the Mac, you can browse photos from the File Browser in the Editor workspace.

In Windows, go to the Editor workspace from the Organizer by choosing File > Browse Folders in Editor. You can also select either Quickly Fix Photos or Edit and Enhance Photos from the welcome screen. If you're already in the Editor workspace, select File > Browse Folders. Figure 8.8 shows the File Browser on Windows.

Figure 8.8
Photoshop Elements File
Browser in Windows

On a Mac, choose Open File for Editing from the welcome screen or go to File > Browse Folders in the top menu.

All these tools help you sort through your digital files so you can group them any way you want. Put all the photos, scanned items, page backgrounds, and clip art for a scrapbook page together or make folders of photographs by date taken or by subject. You can organize your files more easily and with many more options using Photoshop Elements than using the traditional method of putting pieces of paper into envelopes.

Photoshop Elements Editing Tools and Palettes

You need to understand the *interface* in Photoshop Elements to use the program effectively. The interface includes all the different editing modes, tools, palettes, dialog boxes and windows for changing and creating images. In Windows, Photoshop Elements 3 includes three editing *modes*: Auto Fix mode in the Organizer workspace and both Quick Fix mode and Standard Edit mode in the Editor workspace. On the Mac, you have two editing modes: Quick Fix and Standard Edit.

Auto Fix in the Organizer (Windows)

From the Organizer workspace in Windows, you can select and trim a photo and then make some quick automatic changes (see Figure 8.9).

Figure 8.9
The Organizer Auto
Fix window

Follow these steps:
1. Click the Edit icon, and choose the Auto Fix Window.
2. Click any of the general fixes to see the changes.
3. Use the Crop tool to trim your photo.
4. Click Reset Image to undo any changes.

Tip: The Auto Fix features may work on one photo and not the next. These are limited photo fixes, and we recommend using the Editor workspace for photo corrections, as well as for more creative projects.

Editor Workspace Photo Fixing

You can open the Editor workspace in Windows from the Organizer or from the initial welcome screen. From the Organizer, click the Edit icon and choose Go to Quick Fix or Go to Standard Edit. From the initial welcome screen, choose either Quickly Fix Photos or Edit and Enhance Photos. On a Mac, Photoshop Elements automatically opens in the Editor workspace.

Both the Quick Fix and the Standard Edit modes have a Photo Bin on the bottom that shows the open photos. You can close it if you need more desktop area. Both modes include a shortcuts menu bar, a tool options bar, a toolbox, and a column of palettes. The Standard Edit mode offers a greater number of tools and more options for using them.

Quick Fix Mode

The Quick Fix mode offers simple photo fixes such as removing red-eye, making color changes, sharpening images, and cropping pictures, and it allows you to see a side-by-side comparison of the "before" and "after" photos. See Figure 8.10.

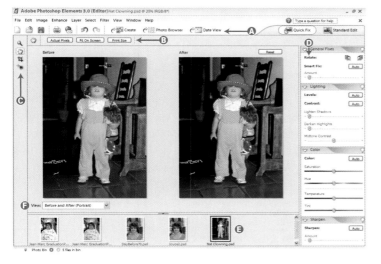

Figure 8.10

Quick Fix mode

Ⓐ (Shortcuts bar)

Ⓑ (Tool options bar)

Ⓒ (Toolbar)

Ⓓ (Photo-fixing palettes)

Ⓔ (Photo Bin)

Ⓕ (View)

In Quick Fix mode, click a photo in the Photo Bin, or go to File > Open and navigate to open an image. Click the View pull down menu, and choose Before and After (Portrait or Landscape). Make changes to the images by clicking the Auto buttons or by moving the sliders in the palettes. To undo any change, click the blue Undo arrow in the shortcuts bar.

Standard Edit Mode

Standard Edit mode (Figure 8.11) has many more tools and options. You can still fix red-eye, adjust colors, and crop pictures, but you can also design original pages and control all the adjustments you make.

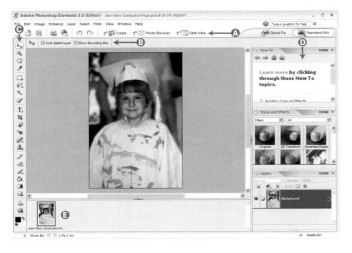

Figure 8.11

Standard Edit mode

Ⓐ (Shortcuts bar)

Ⓑ (Tool options bar)

Ⓒ (Toolbar)

Ⓓ (Palette Bin palettes)

Ⓔ (Photo Bin)

The Toolbar and Its Tools

As with the four tools in the Quick Fix mode, selecting any tool in the Standard Edit mode opens different choices in the options bar. Tools with a little black triangle by them reveal additional tools, and holding the cursor over the tool shows its name and a shortcut key. Table 8.1 provides a quick reference. Regardless of what tools you've used and how many changes you've made, you can always go back to the last saved version of your image by selecting Edit > Revert to Saved, from the main title bar.

▶ **Table 8.1** Elements' Main Tools

Icon	Tool	Keyboard Shortcut	Description
	Move	V	Moves selected areas of your image. You can also drag selections into other images.
	Zoom	Z	Zooms in or out of areas on your image so you can magnify areas on which you want to work.
	Hand	H	Pans over an image so you can see hidden areas in the window.
	Eyedropper	I	Samples colors in an image or anywhere on your screen. Use the sampled color to draw, paint, or match different areas in an image.
	Rectangular Marquee	M	Makes a selection of an area. You can then paint, retouch, move, or apply effects to the selected area without modifying the area outside the selection.
	Elliptical Marquee	M	
	Lasso	L	Lasso draws a freehand selection around an area.
	Magnetic Lasso	L	Magnetic Lasso draws a selection border that snaps to the edges of contrasting colors in an image.
	Polygonal Lasso	L	Polygonal Lasso draws a straight-edged selection border around an area.
	Magic Wand	W	Selects parts of an image based on the similarity of adjacent pixels. Reducing or increasing the Tolerance setting (default 32) in the options bar reduces or increases the range of colors selected.
	Selection Brush	A	Selects an area of your image using your choice of brushes.
	Horizontal Type	T	Type tools enter type in your image. Choose the font attributes in the options bar.
	Vertical Type	T	
	Horizontal Type Mask	T	Type Mask tools create a selection border in the shape of type in your image. Choose the font attributes in the options bar.
	Vertical Type Mask	T	
	Crop	C	Trims off the unselected area of an image. Includes presets in standard photo sizes.
	Cookie Cutter	Q	Creates punch-outs of photos, or colored areas, with many different shapes.

Continued on next page

Icon	Tool	Keyboard Shortcut	Description
	Red Eye Removal	Y	Fixes red-eye with one click.
	Spot Healing Brush	J	The Spot Healing Brush fixes small areas in one click.
	Healing Brush	J	The Healing Brush paints to repair larger scratches and defects or remove entire objects from the photo.
	Clone Stamp	S	Clone Stamp creates a clone so you can copy it to another area or remove unwanted objects.
	Pattern Stamp	S	Pattern Stamp creates a pattern from the selection that you can then stamp into different areas.
	Pencil	N	Draws hard-edged freehand lines.
	Eraser	E	Eraser erases like a normal eraser.
	Background Eraser	E	Background Eraser erases pixels on a layer to transparency.
	Magic Eraser	E	Magic Eraser erases all similar pixels in an area with one click.
	Brush	B	Brush paints with a variety of brush tips. You can sketch and colorize photographs.
	Impressionist Brush	B	Impressionist Brush changes existing colors and details so a photo looks like it was painted with impressionist-styled strokes.
	Color Replacement Brush	B	Color Replacement Brush replaces specific colors in an image with a different color.
	Paint Bucket	K	Fills a selected area with a color or a pattern.
	Gradient	G	Creates a gradual blend from one color to another or across many colors. The options bar has a number of gradient styles.
	Rectangle	U	Draws a variety of predefined shapes.
	Rounded Rectangle	U	
	Ellipse	U	
	Polygon	U	
	Line	U	
	Custom Shape	U	The Custom Shape tool has additional shapes available from the pull-down menu in the options bar
	Shape Selection	U	The Shape Selection tool selects a shape with one click
	Blur	R	Blur softens hard edges.
	Sharpen	R	Sharpen increases clarity of soft edges

Continued on next page

Icon	Tool	Keyboard Shortcut	Description
	Smudge	R	Smudge simulates the action of dragging a finger through wet paint.
	Sponge	O	Sponge changes the color saturation of an area.
	Dodge	O	Dodge lightens areas to bring out details in shadows.
	Burn	O	Burn darkens areas to bring out details in highlights.
	Switches Foreground/Background Colors	X	Switches foreground and background colors.
	Switches Foreground/Background Colors	D	Resets default black foreground and white background.

Standard Edit Mode Palettes

The palettes in the Palette Bin are visual shortcuts to many menu items. Only three of these palettes are visible when you first open Standard Edit: How To, Styles and Effects, and Layers. Select > Window in the main menu and pull down to open other palettes.

Open any of these palettes, and drag them into the Palette Bin. You can also change the order of the palettes by dragging them up or down in the Palette Bin. You'll use the How To palette to follow along with a particular technique, but you may want to keep this palette closed to save room. Click the white triangle by the palette's name to close it temporarily. You'll use the Layers palette often for scrapbooking projects, along with the Styles and Effects, Colors Swatches, and Undo History palettes. Undo History tracks your steps as you change a photo or design a page. Use this palette to step backward and forward to review how you created any part.

Layers Palette Features

The Layers palette is the key to creating many of the special effects that are so easy and fun with Photoshop Elements. Figure 8.12 identifies the controls for the layers.

Figure 8.13

The Layers palette

Ⓐ Blending mode

Ⓑ Layer opacity

Ⓒ Create a new layer

Ⓓ Create adjustment layer

Ⓔ Delete layer

Ⓕ Lock transparent pixels

Ⓖ Lock all

Ⓗ Type layer indicator

Ⓘ Layer visibility indicator

Ⓙ Linked layer indicator

Ⓚ Painting (active) layer indicator

Blending mode determines how the image (pixels) in a layer blends with the image (pixels) in layers beneath it.

Layer opacity changes the opacity of the layer so that more (or less) of the underlying image is visible.

Create a new layer adds an empty layer like a transparent sheet of glass. You can paint items, and they'll be seen on top of the underlying layer. You can also duplicate an existing layer by dragging the layer over this icon.

Create adjustment layer adds a special kind of layer that lets you experiment with color and adjust tones. An adjustment layer acts like a veil, changing how the underlying layer is seen.

Delete layer deletes the active layer. You can also drag a layer on top of the trashcan icon to delete the layer.

Lock transparent pixels locks only the transparent areas of the layer so that you can paint or edit the opaque areas.

Lock all locks all the layer properties. A fully locked layer can't be edited or changed.

Type layer indicator shows a layer with fully editable type.

Layer visibility indicator turns a layer's visibility on or off.

Linked layer indicator shows if a layer is linked to the painting (active) layer.

Painting (active) layer indicator shows the layer that's currently being painted or changed.

Tips for Working with Layers

As you work on photos or projects, you'll add many layers. Here are a few tips to help you with the layers palette:

- To change the thumbnails size, click the MORE pull-out triangle on the Layers palette and select Palette Options.

- To change the order of the layers within the Layers palette, drag one layer above or below the other.

- To move the Background layer or to move a layer below it, you have to rename the Background layer.

- To rename any layer, double-click the layer's name.

One Last Thought…

Getting familiar with any new tool involves learning all its parts and trying it. Take Photoshop Elements for a test spin. Browse through the welcome screen, check out the Organizer, and use the Browser. Organize a sample set of photos, or create a CD contact sheet. Open a digital photo in the Quick Fix mode of the Editor workspace, and apply some changes. Then go to the Standard Edit mode, and try other photo fixes. Photoshop Elements 3 is so much more than a new cropping tool. It's the key to a whole new world of scrapbooking techniques.

Photo Effects

You can easily turn a faded photo into a sepia tone, remove red-eye, or make other changes to improve snapshots and scans for your scrapbooks. Photoshop Elements 3 has two modes for enhancing digital images, the Quick Fix mode and the Standard Edit mode. From the welcome screen in Windows, select Quickly Fix Photos to launch the Quick Fix mode or choose Edit and Enhance Photos to open the Standard Edit mode. On the Mac, Elements opens directly into the Editor workspace where you can choose either mode from the top menu. In this chapter, we'll use some basic photo improvements in the Quick Fix mode and then show how easy it is to make more specific enhancements and special crops using the Standard Edit mode.

9

Chapter Contents

Quick photo fixes
Simple photo retouching in Standard Edit mode
Cropping techniques in Standard Edit mode

Quick Photo Fixes

Use the Quick Fix mode for the simplest photo enhancements. As you become familiar with the tools, you may find different or better ways of changing color, cropping, and more.

Note: Every photo enhancement or design can be done more than one way with Photoshop Elements.

For each exercise in this chapter, you'll need to launch Photoshop Elements first and then perform the following steps depending on your system.

For Windows:

1. Select Quickly Fix Photos from the welcome screen.
2. Choose the Open folder icon.
3. Navigate to the photo, and double-click to open it.

For a Mac:

1. Select Open File for Editing from the welcome screen.
2. Navigate to the photo, and double-click to open it.
3. Click Quick Fix.

After changing each image, select File > Save As and save the file with a new name.

Getting Rid of Red-Eye

Although many newer digital cameras automatically correct red-eye, your scans of film photos and other photographs may still have this unwanted phenomenon. The demonic look of red-eye is actually the reflection on the back of the eye from a camera flash.

To remove red-eye, follow these steps:

1. Select View > Before and After (Portrait or Landscape), as in Figure 9.1.

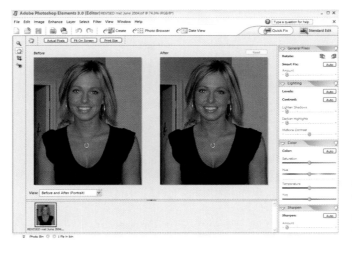

Figure 9.1

View Before and After (Portrait) with red-eye tool and options

2. Use the Zoom tool to drag over both eyes on the After photo.
3. Select the Red-Eye Removal tool. The cursor becomes a crosshair.
4. Reduce the Darken Amount setting in the options bar to about 15 percent, depending how dark you want the eye area.

5. Click in the center of the red-eye for each eye. See the finished photo in Figure 9.2.

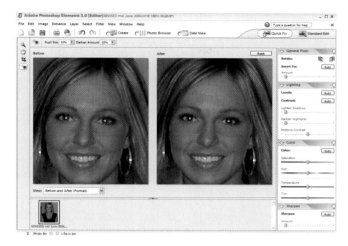

Figure 9.2
Enlarged view with red-eye removed

Making Quick Photo Enhancements

Photos from both film cameras and digital cameras may need some simple color corrections and sharpening. You'll need to experiment, as each photograph is different. The Auto settings apply changes the software assumes are correct. Your choice will depend on the image itself and how you intend to use it.

1. Select View > Before and After (Portrait or Landscape).

2. In the General Fixes palette, rotate the photo if necessary.

3. In the General Fixes palette, try clicking Auto to see if the After image is better than the Before image, as in Figure 9.3.

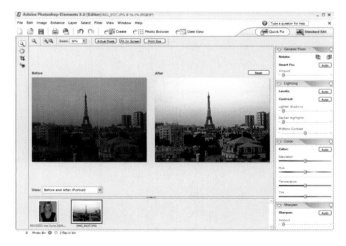

Figure 9.3
General Fixes palette's Auto feature

4. Click Reset, and try the Auto Levels, Auto Contrast, or Auto Color setting, resetting the image after each test.

- Auto Levels increases the contrast and adjusts the colors.
- Auto Contrast increases the contrast without changing colors.
- Auto Color tries to improve the color and the contrast.

5. Click Reset, and apply the settings you liked best.

6. Select the Zoom tool, and click Actual Pixels in the options bar to see a 100 percent view of the image.

7. Click Auto in the Sharpen palette, as shown in Figure 9.4.

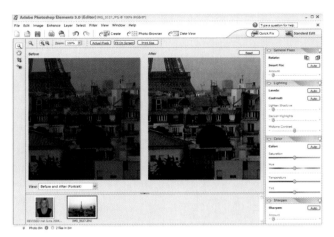

Figure 9.4
100 percent view of sharpened image side by side

 Tip: Always apply sharpening last, after you've made all the other corrections to the photo.

Changing a Photo from Color to Black-and-White or Sepia Tone

Sometimes a black-and-white or sepia-toned photo may best fit the theme of a page or may improve a scan of a very faded photo. Try this quick, easy method:

1. Select View > Before and After (Portrait or Landscape).

2. In the Color palette, move the Saturation slider all the way to the left. Click the check mark to commit this change. See Figure 9.5. Don't worry; it's not permanent until you save the file. You can always click Reset if you change your mind.

Figure 9.5
A black-and-white conversion using the Saturation slider

3. Click Auto in the General Fixes palette to see if it improves the range of tones of white, black, and grays.

4. For a sepia tone, move the Temperature slider in the Color palette slowly to the right, until you have a pleasing sepia tone. Click the check mark to commit this change. See Figure 9.6.

Figure 9.6

Easily turn a black-and-white photo into a sepia-toned image

Quick Photo Cropping

You may want to add interest to a photograph by centering the subject or just removing some unwanted areas. You can use the Crop tool in the Quick Fix mode.

1. Select View > Before and After.

2. Select the Crop tool. (To use the settings in the options bar, check the guidelines in the "Using the Crop Tool" section later in this chapter.)

3. Click and drag out the area on the After image, as in Figure 9.7.

Tip: While continuing to hold down the mouse button, you can reposition the selection by also holding down the spacebar. After you let go of the mouse button and the spacebar, pull on the corners of the selected area to enlarge or reduce the cropped area before committing the change.

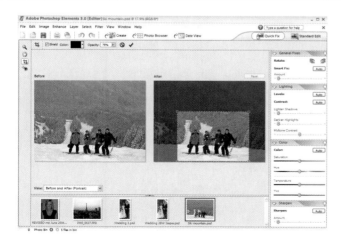

Figure 9.7

A quick crop using the cropping tool

4. When the photo is the size you want, click the check mark to commit the change.

Guidelines for Image Size and Resolution

All digital images have both physical and pixel dimensions. Physical dimensions are the width and height in inches (or centimeters). Pixel dimensions are the pixels/inch of the width and height. The greater the number of pixels/inch in each direction, called the *resolution* of the image, the more data is in the file and the larger the overall file size. A 5×7-inch digital photo with a resolution of 300 pixels/inch will create a larger file than the same photo with a resolution of 72 pixels/inch. Your monitor requires only 72 or 96 pixels per inch to display an image, so the image may look fine on your monitor, but it could be pixilated or blurry when you print.

For scrapbooking, 300 pixels/inch is the optimum resolution for printing and archiving a digital file. Always scan photos so that the finished scan has the physical dimensions you need at 300 pixels/inch. Most digital photos straight from the camera have very large dimensions at 72 pixels/inch. The resolution for clip art will vary. Before enhancing or cropping any image, always check the image size and set the resolution to 300 pixels/inch as follows:

1. Open the image in Photoshop Elements.

2. Go to Image > Resize > Image Size. The current Pixel Dimensions setting shows the width and height in pixels and the file size in megabytes. The current Document Size setting shows the width and height in inches and the resolution in pixels/inch. (You can choose inches or other measurements as defaults by selecting Edit > Preferences > Units & Rulers).

3. Uncheck the Resample Image box to link the resolution to the width and height.

4. Type **300** in the Resolution box. Notice that the width and height adjust accordingly.

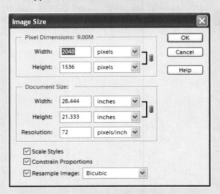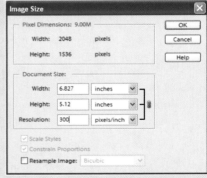

5. Click OK to make this change, as it doesn't affect the existing quality of the image.

Once your image has a resolution of 300 ppi, you can reduce the size by cropping in Photoshop Elements or changing the pixel dimensions in the Image Size dialog box. Changing the pixel dimensions of an image while maintaining the same pixels per inch is called *resampling*. You can downsample, or make the image smaller at the same resolution without noticeably changing the quality of your image. However, to enlarge the image while maintaining the resolution of 300 ppi, use the following steps for the best results. Upsampling makes the software fill in areas or

Continued

interpolate with made-up pixels. Most professional photographers have found that upsampling in small steps using the bicubic smoother method of interpolation preserves the image quality.

1. Select Image > Resize > Image Size.

2. Check the Resample Image box to unlink the width and height from the resolution.

3. Click and hold the Resample Image pull-down menu, and choose *Bicubic Smoother*.

4. Click and hold the width to change it from inches to percent.

5. Increase the percent to 110 percent. Click OK.

6. Select Image > Resize > Image Size again to check the new dimensions.

7. Repeat steps 2 though 6 until the image is the size you need at 300 ppi.

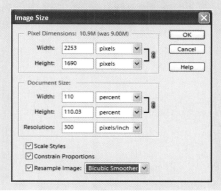

Simple Photo Retouching in Standard Edit Mode

The Standard Edit mode opens a whole set of tools to spark your creativity. In this mode you can whiten teeth, touch up blemishes, sharpen with more control, and make other changes to improve your scrapbook photographs. You can also crop any image more easily than with traditional tools. The following sections show only some of the possibilities. Always save the retouched images by selecting File > Save As to save the file with a new name.

Making Selections

Many of the projects you'll do with Photoshop Elements involve selecting areas of the photo to work on them. You have many ways to select, and the method you use may depend on the photo itself. Open any image to try the following three methods.

> **Note:** A selection is indicated by "marching ants," a moving dashed line around the area. To temporarily hide the lines while keeping the area selected, press Ctrl+H / ⌘ +H. Pressing the same keys again makes the marching ants reappear. Pressing Ctrl+D / ⌘ +D deselects everything.

Before selecting an area, use the Zoom tool to click and drag across the area to have a larger view.

Tip: Using a pen tablet instead of a mouse makes selecting areas much easier and more precise.

With many photo enhancements, you'll want to *feather* the selection. Feathering softens the edge around the part you're changing so the change won't seem unnaturally abrupt. With an area selected, choose Select > Feather in the top menu, and select a one-pixel to five-pixel feather depending on the type and size of area selected.

Method 1: Using the Lasso

As shown in Figure 9.8, you can use the Lasso tool (A) to click and draw around the outside edges of the area. To add to a selection, click the Add to Selection box (B) in the options bar menu. To subtract from the selection, click the Subtract boxes (C).

The following are alternate lassos:

- Use the Magnetic Lasso tool (D) if the picture has strong contrasts around the areas you want to select.
- Use the Polygonal Lasso tool (E) if you're selecting straight edges, clicking each time an edge changes directions.

Note: The Magnetic Lasso and Polygonal Lasso tools will continue to select until you either come back to the original starting spot or Ctrl+click / ⌘ +click.

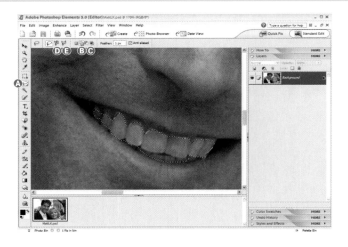

Figure 9.8
Lasso tools and options menu bar

Method 2: Using the Magic Wand

You can also use the Magic Wand tool to select by clicking an area composed of one color (Figure 9.9). The Magic Wand tool works best on solid-colored areas, as the software finds adjoining pixels within a specific color range. Lower the Tolerance setting in the options bar from 32, and the Magic Wand tool selects a smaller color range. Again you can add and subtract from the selection using the Add and Subtract boxes in the options bar.

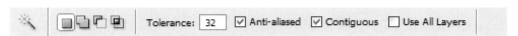

Figure 9.9 Magic Wand tool and options menu bar

Method 3: Using the Selection Brush Tool

The Selection Brush tool is the longest to describe but the easiest method to apply. See Figure 9.10.

1. Use the Selection Brush tool (A), and make some changes in the options menu bar.

   a. Choose a small, soft, round brush, such as a 13-pixel brush. The soft brushes are the ones that look fuzzy in the Brush pull-down menu (B).

   b. Change the Mode setting (C) from Selection to Mask.

   c. Set the Hardness setting (D) to 0%.

   d. Change the Overlay Opacity setting (E) to 20%.

   e. Leave the Overlay Color setting (F) at the default red unless you're selecting something that's red, in which case click the pull-down menu and choose a contrasting color.

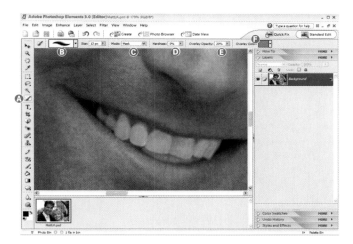

Figure 9.10
Selection Brush tools and options menu bar

2. Paint over the area you want to select until the area is completely covered with the mask color.

Tip: Change any brush size using the bracket keys: [makes a brush smaller and] makes a brush larger.

3. In the options bar, change the Mode setting (C) back to Selection. If any parts are missing from the selection, go back to Mask mode and just paint them in. To remove an area from the selection, hold down Alt/Option and paint over the area.

4. When your selection is complete, choose Select > Inverse to reverse the masked-out area and have only the chosen area selected.

Whitening Teeth

Just whitening a person's teeth in a photo can make the picture sparkle. It's really easy to do with Photoshop Elements.

1. Open the image, and use the Zoom tool to click and drag across the teeth.

2. Make a selection of just the teeth using any selection method.

3. Choose Select > Feather. Choose 1 pixel for the Feather Radius setting.

4. Press Ctrl+H / ⌘ +H to temporarily hide the "marching ants."

5. Using the Zoom tool, zoom out until you can see the whole face. Choose the Zoom Out option in the options bar (the minus sign in the magnifying glass), or use the Zoom slider.

6. In the top menu, select Enhance > Adjust Color > Adjust Hue/ Saturation. Move the dialog box so you can see the teeth as you do the next steps.

7. From the Edit pull-down menu in the Hue/Saturation dialog box, change Master to Yellows. Drag the Saturation slider left to about -50 to remove the yellow. The amount will depend on the person's teeth, and they may look a little green at this point. Don't click OK yet.

8. Still in the Hue/Saturation window, pull down the Edit box again to go back to Master. Slowly drag the Lightness slider to the right until the teeth look whiter but still natural. See Figure 9.11.

9. When the teeth look natural, click OK in the Hue/Saturation window.

10. Deselect the teeth by pressing Ctrl+D / ⌘ +D.

Figure 9.11 The settings in the Hue/Saturation dialog box

Retouching Blemishes

Whether it's a scratch or a pimple, there's no need to save that for posterity.

1. Open the image, and use the Zoom tool to click and drag across the area to enlarge the area you want to touch up.

2. Select the Spot Healing Brush tool (A) shown in Figure 9.12.

3. In the options bar, choose a soft, round brush (B) and a size that's a little larger than the spot you want to remove. Leave the Type choice at Proximity Match.

4. Click the spot you want to remove. That's it!

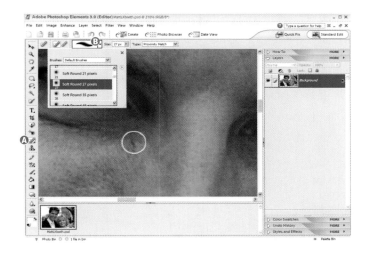

Figure 9.12
The Spot Healing Brush tool and options bar

 Sharpening

Most digital photos and scanned photos will benefit from a little sharpening. Follow these guidelines to get the best result:

- Always apply sharpening last. Make all your color changes and fixes before you sharpen.
- Always zoom the image to 100 percent.
- Sharpen lightly, and repeat if necessary.
- Don't go too far. Watch for little halos around the high-contrast edges in your photo from oversharpening. See Figure 9.13.

Figure 9.13
Avoid the halos of over-sharpening.

To sharpen, follow these steps:

1. Select Filter > Sharpen > Unsharp Mask.

> **Note:** Unsharp Mask sounds like the reverse of what you want to do, but it's the tool for sharpening digital photographs. The name comes from the traditional darkroom technique of sharpening edges.

2. You have three choices to enter. See Figure 9.14.

The **Amount** setting is the amount of sharpening. A higher percent means neighboring pixels will have a stronger effect on one another.

The **Radius** setting is the distance from an edge in pixels that will be affected. A high Amount setting requires a low Radius number.

The **Threshold** setting acts as a damper. The higher the number, the softer the effect. Since the tendency is to oversharpen, it's best to start with a subtle amount of sharpening. The following settings are in the range recommended by many Photoshop instructors and work well for general snapshots.

For subtle sharpening, try using the following settings:

- Amount: 100%; Radius: 1; Threshold: 10

For general sharpening, try using the following settings:

- Amount: 85%; Radius: 1; Threshold: 4

3. Click OK to apply the Unsharp Mask setting.

Figure 9.14
Previewing at 100 percent with a general sharpening applied

Cropping Techniques in Standard Edit Mode

Photoshop Elements has many tools for cropping images, including the new Cookie Cutter tool designed with scrapbookers in mind.

Using the Crop Tool

In both the Quick Fix mode and the Standard Edit mode, you can use the Crop tool to trim your photos. Use this tool freehand by dragging across your photo, or constrain the dimensions and the pixels in the options bar. Always check the image size first, as described earlier in this chapter.

1. Select the Crop tool, and set the width, height, and resolution in the options bar.

Note: You can't use the Crop tool on a small 2×3-inch photo at 72 pixels/inch and expect to get a good quality 4×6-inch photo at 300 pixels/inch. The computer will make up pixels to fill in, but your photo will look…well, pixelated or blurry.

2. Click and drag across the image to highlight the section you want to keep. Move or resize it with the corner boxes.

Tip: You can drag out a perfect square by holding the Shift key as you drag a selection.

3. To rotate the selection, move the cursor just outside the selection area on one of the sides. When the arrow changes to a double-headed curved arrow, click and drag to rotate the selection, as in Figure 9.15.

4. Click the check mark in the options bar to commit the crop, or click the cancel symbol. Even after you make the crop, you can change your mind and go back to the original by clicking the left blue Undo arrow in the shortcuts bar.

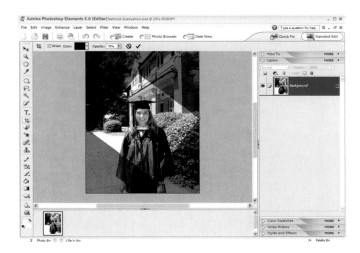

Figure 9.15
Rotating a crop with the
Crop tool

Cropping with the Marquee Tool

Using either the Rectangular or the Elliptical Marquee tool, you can create various geometric shapes from your photo. You'll save ink costs when printing on an ink-jet printer, as you'll print only the part your want to place on your page. And cutting out a printed shape is much easier.

1. Open an image, and select the Elliptical Marquee tool.

2. Click and drag across your photo to select the portion you want to keep.

> **Tip:** Add the space bar as you click and drag to move the selection to the precise area. Then release the space bar only and continue to enlarge or reduce the size of the selection.

3. You can enlarge the selection as long as you continue to depress the mouse button.

4. Release the mouse button, and the area will be selected.

5. Ctrl+J / ⌘ +J to jump the selection onto a new layer. Your window won't look different since your original photo is still visible.

6. Click on the Background layer in the Layers palette.

7. Select Edit > Fill Layer, and select white or a color from the Use menu.

8. Click OK. The background layer will fill with the selected color, as in Figure 9.16.

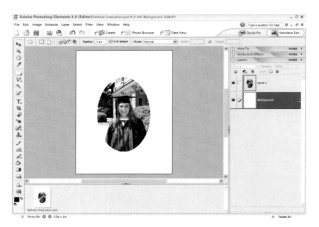

Figure 9.16
An oval marquee crop

Using the Cookie Cutter Tool

The Cookie Cutter tool offers even more possibilities for scrapbookers and includes a variety of cropping shapes.

1. Open a photo to crop.

2. Select the Cookie Cutter tool (A) on the toolbar and make some changes in the options bar. See Figure 9.17

   a. Click the pull-down menu (B) next to the heart shape in the options bar. You'll see 30 different shapes you can use.

   b. Click the tiny triangle in a circle (C) on the right side of the pull-down menu.

   c. Select All Elements Shapes. You will now have more than 500 shapes to use! The black areas in each shape represent the part of your picture that will remain. The white parts will be cut away.

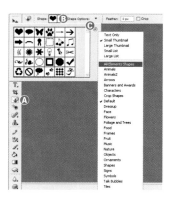

Figure 9.17
More cookie cutter choices

3. Choose a shape from the options bar.

4. Click and drag the cursor over the part of the photo you want to keep.

5. Release the mouse button or lift the stylus pen. Your cropped photo will be on a light-gray checkerboard, as in Figure 9.18.

Note: The light-gray checkerboard on any layer indicates transparent areas.

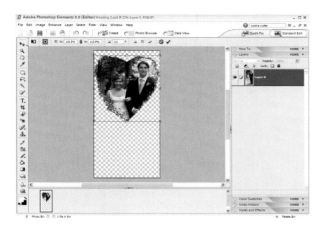

Figure 9.18
Using the Cookie Cutter tool makes photo cropping more creative.

6. To adjust the position of the shape relative to the photo, click in the center and move it around.

7. To adjust the size of the shape, pull in or out on the square anchor points.

8. To rotate the shape relative to the photo, place the cursor just outside the shape. The cursor turns into a curved double-headed arrow. Click and drag the shape.

9. Click the check mark in the options bar to commit the crop.

Creating Punch Shapes

You can create one large colored punch-out to use on a digital page, or fill a page with different shapes to print and cut with scissors at your next crop.

1. From the File menu, choose New > Blank File.

2. In the New dialog box, select a page size and choose 300 pixels/inch for the resolution to be consistent. See Figure 9.19.

Figure 9.19
The New dialog box choices

3. Click the Foreground color box in the toolbox, and select a color.

4. Select the Paint Bucket tool, and click in the new blank page. The whole page fills with color.

> **Tip:** Turn on rulers for any image. Go to View > Rulers, or press Ctrl+R / ⌘ +R.

5. Select the Cookie Cutter tool and a shape from the Shape pull-down menu in the options bar.

6. Click and drag the shape on the colored page, as in Figure 9.20.

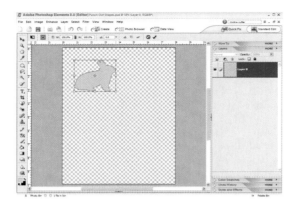

Figure 9.20
A bunny shape punch-out

7. Click the check mark in the options bar to commit the shape.

8. Use the Move tool to change the size or rotate the shape.

9. Click the check mark to apply any changes.

10. Ctrl+click / ⌘ +click the New Layer icon in the Layers palette to put a new layer below the layer with the shape, now named Layer 0.

11. Go to Edit > Fill Layer, and choose a color to fill the empty layer.

Creating Multiple Copies of One Shape

Make multiple copies of this shape at different sizes on one page.

1. In the Layers palette, click the Shape layer and drag it over the New Layer icon.

2. Use the Move tool to move the punch-out shape on the new layer so that it doesn't overlap the original one. Resize or rotate it if you want.

3. Repeat steps 1 and 2 to fill the page. See Figure 9.21.

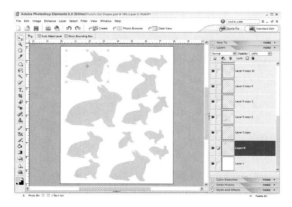

Figure 9.21
Pink bunnies everywhere

Creating Different Shapes on the Same Page

Fill the page with different punch-out shapes and even different-colored shapes.

1. Click the New Layer icon in the Layers palette.

2. Select Edit > Fill Layer, and choose any color.

3. Select another shape, and click and drag it out on the colored layer.

4. Click the check mark to commit the shape.

5. Repeat steps 1 though 4 until you have all the shapes you need.

Adding Layer Styles for Special Effects

Use the layer styles to create punch-out shapes with three-dimensional effects.

1. In the Styles and Effects palette, select Layer Styles in the left pull-down menu.

2. Select a choice from the right pull-down menu, such as Bevels or Wow Plastic.

3. Use the Move tool to click a punch shape, highlighting the layer.

4. Click a bevel or other layer style to apply. You'll see an *f* in a circle on the layer indicating that an effect has been applied. Apply the same or a different layer style to each layer, as in Figure 9.22.

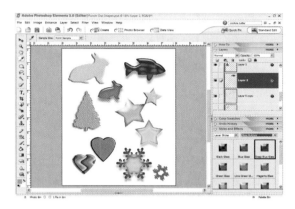

Figure 9.22
Different layer styles on each layer

Finishing and Saving the Punch-out Page

The page filled with punch-out shapes contains many different layers. You can save the file with all the layers or save a "flattened" file. Saving all the layers allows you to copy the individual layers to another image later. Flattening the file combines all the layers and creates a smaller file.

1. Select File > Save As, and save the file with the Save: Layers box checked in the Save Options area. Save as a TIFF (.tif) file.

2. Alternatively, go to Layer > Flatten Image. Then go to File > Save As, and save the flattened image as a TIFF (.tif) file.

> **Note:** Saving the layers in files creates a larger file requiring more storage space.

One Last Thought…

Even if you were to use only the organization of the browser and edit in the Quick Fix mode, Photoshop Elements would be the perfect software for scrapbooking. Use the Standard Edit mode and you can create designs that would be difficult or impossible with traditional scrapbooking tools. We've only scratched the surface of the power of Photoshop Elements. The simplicity of this application makes digital scrapbooking easy, fast, and fun.

Special Effects

You can do so many things with Photoshop Elements; the hard part is deciding which effect to use and when to stop. Elements filters are like walking into the biggest craft supply store in the world and having everything and anything at your fingertips. Just a few clicks of the mouse and some brush strokes with a Wacom stylus, and your photos have frames, or your snapshots become drawings or paintings. The suggested projects in this chapter are only a taste of what's possible.

10

Chapter Contents
Frames and mattes
Artistic effects
Creative effects

Frames and Mattes

Photos with frames or mattes always stand out in a scrapbook. Adding frames in Photoshop Elements is quick and easy. In the Standard Edit mode, select File > Open or File > Browse Folders to open a photo. When you finish any project, make sure to select File > Save As and save the file with a new name.

Creating a Simple Frame or Border

 To create a simple frame or border, follow these steps:

1. In the Styles and Effects palette, choose Effects on the left pull-down menu and Frames on the right pull-down menu. See Figure 10.1.

Figure 10.1
Use the Styles and Effects palette to apply a quick frame.

 Tip: This palette has two types of frames: those that apply a frame directly to the entire photograph and those that require a selection. To make a selection, drag across the photo with the Rectangular Marquee or the Elliptical Marquee tool, or create any other type of selection area. Then apply the frame.

2. Pick a frame effect, and double-click to apply it.

3. Select Layer > Flatten Image before saving. See the samples in Figure 10.2.

Figure 10.2 From left to right, samples of Photo Corners Frame, Recessed Frame, Ripple Frame, and Wood Frame
Photo © Michael Salas

Matching the Frame Color

To make a frame color that matches a color in the photo, follow these steps:

1. Select the Eyedropper tool .

2. In the options bar, set Sample Size to 3 by 3 Average.

3. Use the Eyedropper tool to click a color in the photo, setting the foreground color in the toolbox to match the color in the photo.

4. In the Styles and Effect palette, double-click Foreground Color Frame. See the sample in Figure 10.3.

Figure 10.3
Match the frame color to a color in the photograph.
Photo © Michael Salas

Creating Any Shape Frame or Matte

 To create a shape frame or matte for a photo, follow these steps:

1. Select the Cookie Cutter tool and a solid shape from the pull-down menu in the options bar.

2. Click and drag over your photo to crop the main image.

3. Move and resize the shape to fit your image using the square anchor points. Click the check mark to commit the crop. See Figure 10.4.

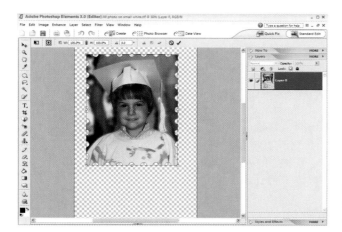

Figure 10.4
Using the Cookie Cutter shape to crop the photo.

4. Ctrl+click / ⌘+click the New Layer icon in the Layers palette to put a new empty layer below the photo layer.

5. Select Image > Resize > Canvas Size.

6. Increase the width and height about 2 inches each in the Canvas Size dialog box. Click OK.

7. Click the foreground color in the toolbox to choose a frame color.

8. Click the empty layer in the Layers palette to highlight it.

9. Select the Paint Bucket tool. Click in the image to fill the layer with color as in Figure 10.5.

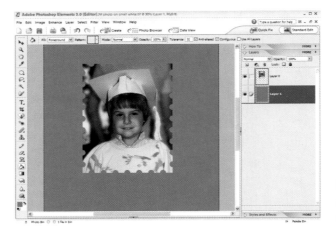

Figure 10.5
Larger Background layer filled with color

10. With the colored layer still highlighted in the Layers palette, select the Cookie Cutter tool and drag out the same shape, creating a border around the photo.

11. Resize the frame using the square anchor points. Click the check mark.

Adding Depth

To add depth variation, follow these steps:

1. Click the bottom layer, Layer 1, in the Layers palette to highlight it.

2. In the Styles and Effects palette, select Layer Styles in the left pull-down and Bevels in the right pull-down menu.

3. Click a bevel to apply it to the "frame" layer, Layer 1.

4. Click the top or "photo layer" in the Layers palette.

5. In the Styles and Effects palette, select Inner Shadows in the right pull-down menu.

6. Click an inner shadow to apply it to the photo layer, as in Figure 10.6.

Figure 10.6
Scalloped Edge Bevel applied to the colored "frame" layer and Inner Shadow Low applied to the photo layer

Tip: With your photo on a layer, you can apply any of the layer styles directly to the photo itself. Inner Bevels, Inner Shadows, and Inner Glows work well when applied directly to a framed photo.

Removing Steps and Styles

To undo one step at a time, click the blue Undo arrow in the shortcuts bar.

To remove layer styles only, right-click / Ctrl+click in the highlighted area in the Layers palette (not on the layer thumbnail) and choose Clear Layer Style.

To go back to your original image, select Edit > Revert to Saved.

Artistic Effects

Even if you think you can't draw a thing, you *can* draw and paint with a computer and Photoshop Elements. Transform photos with different filters and use a Wacom tablet and stylus to apply brush strokes as you would with a real paintbrush. You can also draw and paint on a blank page "from scratch" using Elements brushes and a stylus. Either way, you'll end up with a piece of art and no eraser shreds or paint splatters to clean. And if you don't like your creation, just delete the file. The following sections cover some techniques to get you started.

Creating a Painted Drawing from a Photograph

Make original note cards or painted photos using any image, even a blurred photograph, since this technique works best on a less detailed image. To see the effect as you work, you will need to zoom in to 100 percent on your screen.

1. Select File > Open, and open a photo.
2. Duplicate the Background layer twice by dragging the layer thumbnail over the New Layer icon in the Layers palette and repeating this step a second time.
3. Rename the top layer Outlines by double-clicking the layer name in the Layers palette and entering the new name.
4. Rename the middle layer Painting the same way.
5. Click the visibility (eye) icon in the original Background layer and in the Outlines layer to turn the visibility off temporarily for these two layers.

Your Layers palette should now look like Figure 10.7.

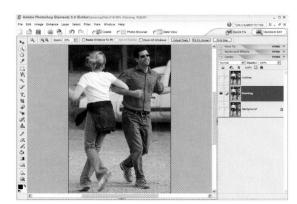

Figure 10.7
The Layers palette ready to create a painted drawing

6. With the middle Painting layer highlighted, select Filter > Blur > Gaussian Blur. Select a Radius of about 5. You want the image to be blurry. Click OK.

7. Still on the Painting layer, select Filter > Artistic > Underpainting.

8. In the Underpainting dialog box, make the following changes, as in Figure 10.8:

   - Brush Size: 12
   - Texture Coverage: 12
   - Texture: Canvas
   - Scaling: 120%
   - Relief: 12

   These settings are good starting points. You may want to choose different settings depending on your photograph. Click OK when you're finished.

Figure 10.8
Underpainting dialog
box settings

9. Click the Outlines layer in the Layers palette to highlight it.

10. Select Enhance > Adjust Color > Remove Color (Figure 10.9). The layer turns into a black-and-white photo.

11. Select Filter > Stylize > Find Edges (Figure 10.10). The top layer turn into an outlined drawing that you'll blend with the Painting layer to finish the painted drawing.

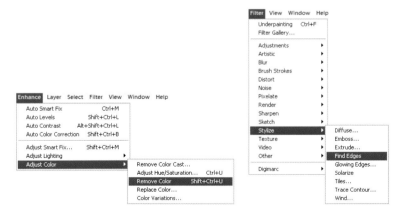

Figure 10.9 Remove Color menu

Figure 10.10 Find Edges menu

12. Use the Zoom tool, and zoom to 100 percent to see the painting at full size.

13. In the Layers palette, change the blending mode of the Outlines layer from Normal to Multiply, and reduce the opacity to about 50 percent, as in Figure 10.11.

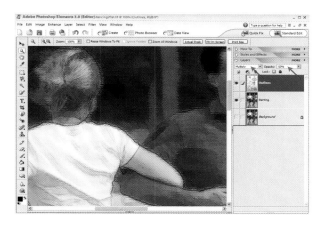

Figure 10.11
Changing the blending mode and layer opacity

14. Drag the original Background layer in the Layers palette to the palette trashcan.

15. Make sure the visibility (eye) icons for both the Painting layer and the Outlines layer are turned on, and select Layer > Flatten Image. Both layers combine into a new Background layer.

16. Click the New Layer icon in the Layers palette to place a blank layer above the Background layer.

17. Select Edit > Fill Layer. In the Contents, choose Use: White. Click OK.

18. In the Layers palette, change the blending mode of the white layer from Normal to Overlay, and reduce the opacity until your photo looks more like a painting.

19. Make sure both layers are turned on, and select Layer > Flatten Image.

20. Select File > Save As, and save your painted drawing with a new name. Figure 10.12 shows the final painted drawing.

Figure 10.12 A photo becomes a painted drawing.

Simple Sketched Photo Look

Making a photograph look as though it were sketched onto the page creates a whole new feeling to your photo and your scrapbook page. Using Photoshop Elements and a Wacom stylus and tablet, you can apply this technique to a regular photo or to one you've already transformed into a painted drawing for an even more "painterly" finished image.

1. Select File > Open, and open a photo or a photo painting.

2. Click the New Layer icon in the Layers palette to place a new blank layer above the Background layer.

3. Set the default foreground and background colors by clicking the letter *D*. Reverse the foreground and background colors by clicking the two-headed arrow next to them in the toolbox .

Note: Click the small black-and-white squares at the bottom of the toolbox to set the default colors. Then reverse these by clicking the two-headed arrow just to the right of the larger black-and-white squares.

4. Select the Paint Bucket tool and click the new blank layer to fill it with white.

5. In the Layers palette, click Opacity and move the slider to fade the white layer just enough so you can see the Background layer below, as in Figure 10.13.

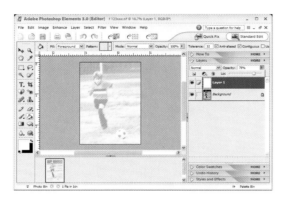

Figure 10.13
Changing the opacity of the white layer

6. Select the Eraser tool, and in the options bar, pull down on the brush presets.

7. Click and hold the default brushes. Highlight Dry Media Brushes. See Figure 10.14.

8. Click the Brush Selection tool again, and choose a brush that looks like a broad stroke of charcoal or any brush that isn't a solid stroke. Figure 10.15 shows the selection of a hard charcoal-edge brush.

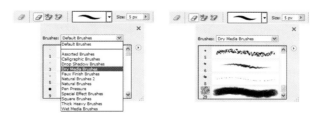

Figure 10.14 Selecting the dry media brushes

Figure 10.15 A hard charcoal-edge brush

9. Click the Size window in the options bar, and drag the slider to the right to increase the brush size.

10. Using the Eraser tool, draw broad strokes across the white layer.

11. When you see enough of your subject, move the Opacity slider for the white layer in the Layers palette back to 100 percent.

12. Continue "sketching" your photo. If you sketch (erase) too much, switch to the Brush tool, making sure you have the same brush style selected and White in the foreground color box, and brush the white back in. See Figure 10.16.

13. When the sketched photo look is finished, select Layer > Flatten Image and then choose File > Save As with a new name. Figure 10.17 shows the final sketch.

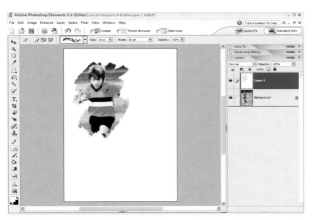

Figure 10.16 Draw broad strokes across the blank layer to reveal the photo underneath.

Figure 10.17 Sketched photo look

Creative Effects

Your imagination is the only limit to what you can do with Photoshop Elements. The following are some simple creative ideas to get you started and make your scrapbook pages unique.

Colorizing a Black-and-White Photo

In the Standard Edit mode, select File > Open, and open a color or black-and-white photo. If your photo is a color photo to start with, convert it to a black-and-white image, using the technique shown in Chapter 9. If it's a black-and-white image, make sure it's in RGB color mode by going to Image > Mode > RGB Color.

1. Click the New Layer icon in the Layers palette to create a new empty layer above your photo layer.

2. With the new layer highlighted, pull down on the left box in the Layers palette to change the layer mode from Normal to Soft Light as in Figure 10.18.

Figure 10.18
Changing the layer mode
to Soft Light

3. Use the Zoom tool to enlarge the area to colorize. You may want to make a selection of the area, using one of the methods described in Chapter 9, before proceeding.

4. Select the Brush tool, and choose a soft, round brush or airbrush the size of the smallest area where you want color.

5. Click the foreground color, and choose a color.

6. Paint carefully over the area you want to colorize.

 Note: This is one of the many times when using a Wacom tablet and stylus makes everything much easier! You can control the stylus as though you were using a traditional paintbrush or airbrush.

7. Change colors, and paint in other areas if you like.

8. Use the Zoom tool to zoom out to see the whole photo.

9. Click the Opacity slider in the Layers palette, and move the slider to the left until the colorization has the effect you want. See Figure 10.19.

Figure 10.19
A colorized black-and-white photo

Creating a Mosaic Photo Effect

Use the mosaic effect to add interest and focus to a snapshot. In the Standard Edit mode, select File > Open, and open the photo.

1. Use the Rectangular Marquee tool to select one of the areas for a "mosaic tile."

2. Click the Add to Selection icon in the options bar.

3. Continue to select areas. It's OK to have these separated or joined depending on your photo and the look you want. The selected areas can be any size or shape, and you can have as many selections as you want.

4. Ctrl+J / ⌘+Shift+J to jump the selections to their own layer. See Figure 10.20.

Figure 10.20
Multiple areas selected and placed on a separate layer

5. In the Styles and Effects palette, select Layer Styles in the left pull-down and Drop Shadows in the right pull-down menu.

6. With the new top layer selected in the Layers palette, click the Low drop shadow.

7. Double-click the Background layer in the Layers palette to change the name from Background to Layer 0, and click OK to apply the name change.

Note: Layer styles can only be applied to a layer. The background isn't officially a layer until you rename it.

8. With Layer 0 highlighted, choose Layer Styles in the left pull-down menu and Image Effects from the right pull-down in the Styles and Effects palette.

9. Click the Fog effect. See Figure 10.21. Try adding text to the "fogged" area to create a unique greeting card.

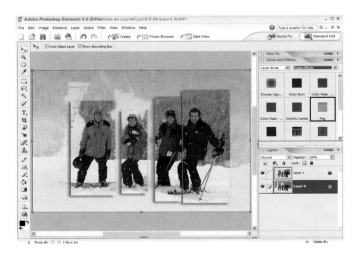

Figure 10.21
The Fog image effect applied to the background

Making a Sports Trading Card

You can create trading cards from any photographs. Print and trade them, or place the cards in a scrapbook. Start by selecting File > Open, to open a photo in the Standard Edit mode. Make sure the photo is set to 300 ppi by selecting Image > Resize > Image Size and following the guidelines in Chapter 9.

1. Select the Crop tool, and set the width and height in the options bar to 1.875 inches by 2.625 inches, respectively. Set the resolution to 300 pixels/inch.

2. Click and drag in the photo to select the main area. Click OK to commit.

 N o t e : Traditional trading cards are 1.875 inches by 2.625 inches.

3. Select the Eyedropper tool. Set the Sample size in the options bar to 3 by 3 Average and click an area of your photo to use as the color for the card.

4. Click the New Document icon, or select File New > Blank File.

5. In the New dialog box, name the file and set the width and height for the card to 1.875 inches by 2.625 inches, respectively. Set the resolution to 300 pixels/inch. Click OK. See Figure 10.22.

Figure 10.22
Settings for a traditional trading card

6. Select the Paint Bucket tool, and click in the new blank document to fill it with the foreground color.

7. In the shortcuts bar, click the Automatically Tile Windows icon to display both files at the same time ⊞. You should see both the photo and the empty card on your screen, as in Figure 10.23.

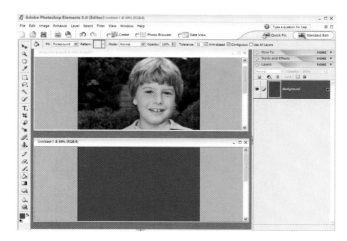

Figure 10.23
Both open files are tiled on the screen.

8. Use the Move tool to click the photo and drag it onto the colored card.

9. Click the Maximize icon in the shortcuts bar to see the whole trading card.

10. Use Move tool, and hold the Shift key down as you pull on the square anchor points to make the photo fit on the trading card.

N o t e : Holding the Shift key down as you resize a photo constrains the proportions.

---

11. Use the Move tool to position the photo on the card, and click the check mark.

12. In the Layers palette, click the photo layer, Layer 1.

13. In the Styles and Effects palette, select Layer Styles on the left and Drop Shadows on the right.

14. Click a drop shadow to apply it to the photo layer.

15. Click the foreground color to select a color for the text.

16. Select the Type tool and type some text on the photo or the card. See Figure 10.24.

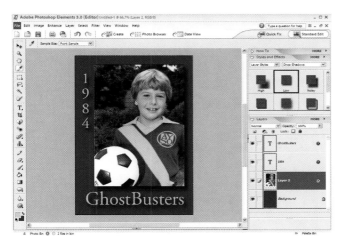

Figure 10.24
The finished trading card is ready to be flattened and printed.

One Last Thought...

Whether you're a natural artist or you just enjoy crafts and scrapbooking, you *can* paint, sketch, and scrapbook more creatively with Photoshop Elements. All the tools and materials are in one place, giving you complete creative freedom. Try all sorts of different looks for your page, and never spend a penny on supplies, on trips to the store, or on transportation to get there. Start with a design, a photo, or nothing at all, and just play with the tools on a white page. Once you start using Photoshop Elements, you won't want to stop.

Text Effects

Photoshop Elements is an image-editing application, yet it includes type tools that turn ordinary words into creative designs. You can type on a blank page in Elements, stylize the letters or words, or add text directly to photos to give your snapshots a unique look. By painting letter forms as images, you can create personalized page toppers or labels. And you can use a photograph to fill the letters of a word or title. The tools in Photoshop Elements can help you create designs that would be difficult or impossible using only traditional tools such as pens and scissors.

11

Chapter Contents

Stylizing editable text
Adding text to photos
Painting text
Filling text with a background or photo

Stylizing Editable Text

 When you type with the Type tools in Photoshop Elements, the letters are placed on a Type layer. The text remains editable as long as you see a *T* in the layer thumbnail. Remove one word or a whole line, or add words and punctuation, and the styles are applied to whatever is added.

1. In the Standard Edit mode, click the New Document icon or select File > New > Blank File. Set the width and height for the scrapbook page, and set the resolution to 300 pixels/inch. Set the color mode to RGB Color, and make the background contents white. Click OK.

2. Select the horizontal (A) or vertical (B) Type tool from the toolbox. See Figure 11.1.

3. In the options bar, choose a font family (C), style (D), and size (E), and then turn on anti-aliasing (F).

Figure 11.1 The options bar for the Type tools

 Note: Anti-aliasing minimizes the jagged appearance of the letters or shapes by partially filling the edge pixels so the edges blend into the background.

You can also choose other text attributes such as faux bold or italic (G), text alignment (H), leading style (I), color (J), layer style (K), text warping (L), and text orientation (M) from the options bar. Set these options now, or wait until you see your text on the page. As long as the text is editable, you can use the Type tool to select a letter, word, or sentence and change the style options.

Note: *Leading* is the space between the lines. The term comes from traditional type setting where little strips of lead were placed between the lines of metal letters. Auto leading results in an extra 20 percent of the point size of the type. For example, auto leading for 10-point type is 12 points. Smaller leading brings the lines of text closer together, and larger leading spreads the lines apart.

4. Click in the blank page to set an insertion point, and type the text. Elements doesn't have automatic text wrapping, so you'll need to press Enter/Return to start a new line.

5. Click the check mark in the options bar to commit the text, or just click another tool. See Figure 11.2. Your text is placed on a Type layer and remains editable.

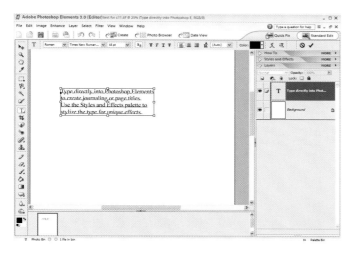

Figure 11.2

Typing text directly into Photoshop Elements

6. Select the Move tool to move and reshape the text. Pull on the corner anchor points to stretch the text as a whole. To maintain the proportions of the letters, hold the Shift key down as you pull on the corners. Click the check mark to commit the changes.

7. Select the Type tool again, and click the warp icon in the options bar.

Note: You can't warp text that has faux bold applied.

8. In the Warp Text dialog box, pull down on the Style menu and choose a warp style, as in Figure 11.3. Make changes to the style using the sliders and Horizontal or Vertical choices. You can see the effects on the text as you try them. To start over, hold the Alt/Option key, which turns the Cancel button into a Reset button. Click Reset, and the dialog box returns to the default settings and your text remains as you typed it.

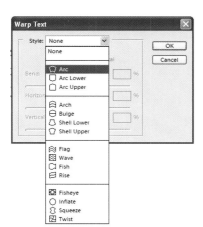
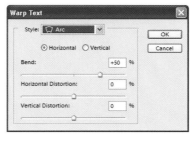

Figure 11.3

The Warp Text dialog box offers many variations for warping text.

9. Once you decide on a warp style, click OK to apply the warp.

10. In the Styles and Effects palette, choose Layer Styles on the left pull-down menu and any option on the right pull-down menu. Click the style thumbnail to apply it.

If the text is journaling, avoid overstylizing and making it unreadable. For a name or title, select any style or combination that fits your page design. See Figure 11.4.

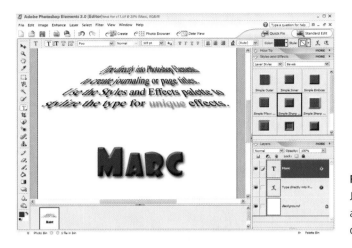

Figure 11.4
Journaling and a title for a page should be stylized differently.

11. Select File > Save As (Ctrl+Shift+S / ⌘+Shift+S) to save the file with the layer and editable text.

Adding Text to Photographs

You can create photo greeting cards, calendar photos, or original scrapbook photos by adding text directly to a photograph.

1. Select File > Open to open the photo.

2. Select the Type tool, position the insertion point where you want the text to start, and type. You don't have to be exact since you can move the text after you enter it. Click the check mark in the options bar to commit the text.

3. Use the Move tool to move the text where you want it on the page, as in Figure 11.5.

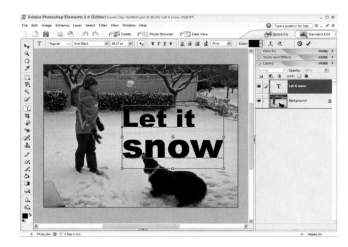

Figure 11.5
Typing directly onto a photograph

4. Select the Type tool again to change the font, the size, the alignment, and the leading to fit your picture.

5. Style the type with the Layer Styles palette. The example in Figure 11.6 uses the font Almont Snow from the ZipArt collection, Font Disk #1, with a Simple Pillow Emboss bevel from the Layer Styles list in the Styles and Effects palette.

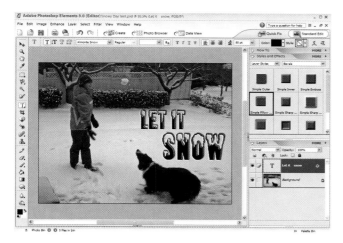

Figure 11.6
An ordinary snapshot becomes an original note card or scrapbook photo

Painting Text

You can create original page toppers, tags, and titles by painting the text. Enter the text, transform it into an image, and use all the tools in Photoshop Elements to create original designs.

Entering the Text

Start by typing the text on a new blank page as in the "Stylizing Editable Text" section.

1. Select File > New > Blank File. Set the width and height for the scrapbook page, and set the resolution to 300 pixels/inch. Set the color mode to RGB Color, and make the background contents white. Click OK.
2. Select the horizontal or vertical Type tool.
3. In the options bar, choose a font family, style, and size and then turn anti-aliasing on.
4. Click in the blank page, and type the text. Warp the text if you want. Click the check mark to commit.
5. Use the Move tool to reshape the text. Click the check mark.

> **Note:** When you use the Type tools to enter text, or use the Cookie Cutter and Custom Shape tools, you're initially drawing *vector graphics*, shapes represented by a mathematical formula. As long as the type and shapes are vector graphics, you can edit the text and scale the letters or forms without stretching pixels.

Simplifying the Layer

Photoshop Elements is an image-editing application, and most of the tools work with *bitmapped* images. Technically known as *raster images*, bitmapped images are filled with pixels. All the digital photographs you open are bitmapped (raster) images. To use the painting tools or the filters in Photoshop Elements, you must change the vector graphics on the layer into raster images by *simplifying* the layer.

Simplifying, or *rasterizing*, a layer changes vector objects into bitmaps so they have the same properties as any photograph. When you simplify a Type layer, the text changes from typed words into a picture of those letter shapes. Simplifying a Shape layer turns the shape into a picture of that shape. To simplify a layer, do one of the following:

- Select Layer > Simplify Layer in the top menu.
- Click the MORE pull-out menu, and choose Simplify Layer from the Layers palette.
- After entering text, select a painting tool, such as the Brush tool, from the toolbox and click in the image. Elements will ask if you want to simplify the layer. Click OK. See Figure 11.7.

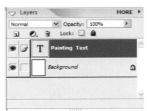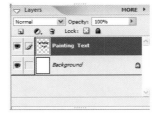

Figure 11.7
Type layer is simplified to use the painting tools.

 Note: You must choose to simplify a Type layer or a custom Shape layer. However, clicking the check mark after using the Cookie Cutter tool automatically simplifies the layer with a cutout.

Coloring Each Letter Individually

If you really want to vary your design, you can give each letter a different color.

1. Click the foreground color in the toolbox.
2. Choose a color from the Color Picker dialog box and click OK.
3. Select the Paint Bucket tool. Make sure Anti-Aliased and Contiguous are checked in the options bar.
4. "Pour" the paint by lining up the paint bucket with the letter you want to fill, and click. (Be sure to line up the small black area coming out of the paint bucket.)
5. Click the foreground color again, change the color in the dialog box, and use the Paint Bucket tool to pour the color on another letter.
6. Repeat step 5 until all the letters are colored. See Figure 11.8.

Filling All the Letters with a Color or a Pattern

You can also use a favorite pattern to fill the letters.

1. Ctrl+click / ⌘+click the layer in the Layers palette to select all the letters.
2. Select Edit > Fill Selection.
3. In the Contents section of the Fill Layer dialog box, click the Use pull-down menu to select Pattern, and click the Custom Pattern menu to choose a pattern. The pull-out arrow in a circle offers many more pattern choices. Click OK.
4. The letters will fill with the chosen pattern, as in Figure 11.9.

Tip: You can add a stroke to any selected text. Choose Edit > Stroke (Outline) Selection. In the Stroke dialog box, choose a width, color, and location for the stroke. Click OK to apply the stroke.

Filling All the Letters with a Gradient

To give your text even more color, you can easily add a gradient.

1. Ctrl+click / ⌘+click the layer in the Layers palette to select all the letters.
2. Select the Gradient tool from the toolbar.
3. Click the Gradient pull-down menu in the options bar to select a color set. The pull-out menu offers many more choices.
4. From the options bar, select a gradient style by clicking one of the five choices.
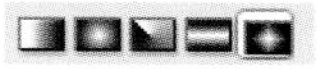
5. Click and drag across the selected letters in any direction. The gradient will fill the letters differently each time. See Figure 11.10.

Applying Layer Styles

Using different layer styles, you can really add variety to your text.

1. In the Styles and Effects palette, choose Layer Styles in the left pull-down menu and any of the options in the right pull-down menu.
2. Click any of the layer style thumbnails to apply the style. Mix and match, and have fun! See Figure 11.11.

Note: You can edit a layer style to customize your design. With a layer style selected, choose Layer > Layer Style > Style Settings. Customize the available choices in the Style Settings dialog box, and click OK.

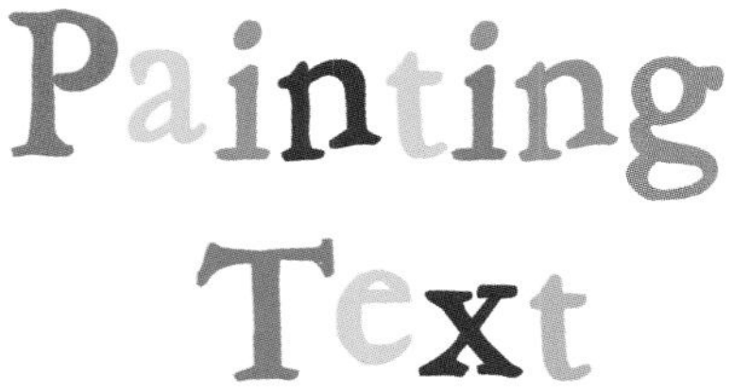

Figure 11.8 Color the letters individually.

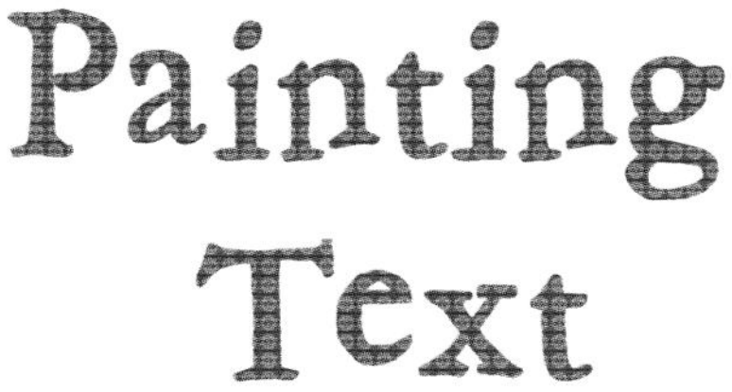

Figure 11.9 Filling text with a pattern

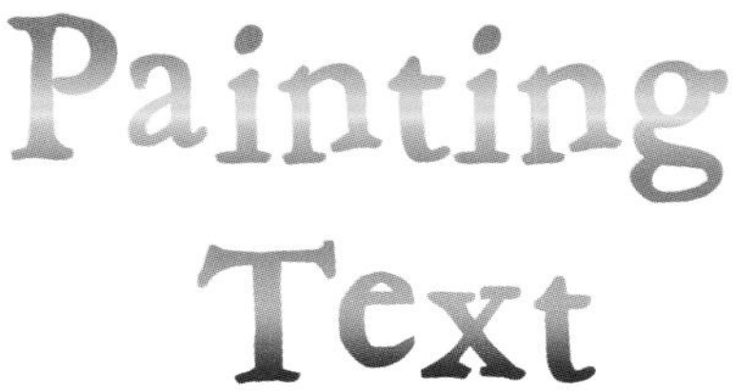

Figure 11.10 Just one of many gradient possibilities

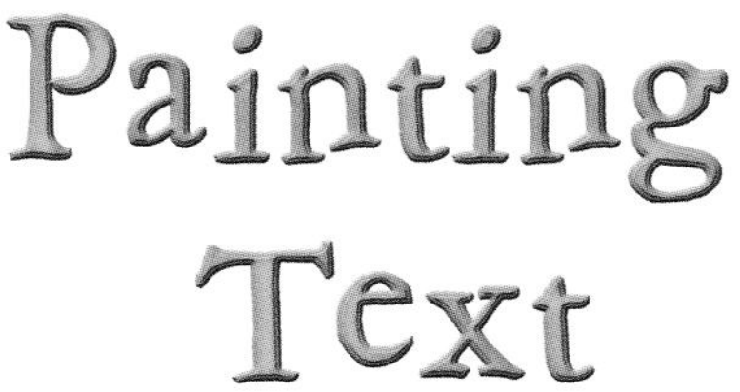

Figure 11.11 You can't do this with pens, paper, and scissors!

Filling Text with a Background or Photo

You've seen photographs filling type in magazines and on television. Using Photoshop Elements you can easily add this effect to your scrapbooks to make truly original title pages.

Creating the Photo-Filled Text

Elements includes a Horizontal and a Vertical Type Mask tool for cutting out selections of the photo underneath. The tool works well as long as you don't move or resize the text once you enter it. The following technique is easier and more flexible:

1. Select File > Open, and choose a photograph. Scenes generally work better than pictures of people.

2. Duplicate the Background layer by dragging it over the New Layer icon in the Layers palette.

3. Select the Horizontal or Vertical Type tool and a large size font in the options bar so the letters will be fat. A sans serif font works best.

4. Click in the image and type. The text is placed on a Type layer. See Figure 11.12.

Figure 11.12
Use a fat font such as Baltar from the ZipArt Font Disk #2.

5. Select the Move tool. Pull and stretch the type to a shape that fits your photo using the square anchors, as in Figure 11.13. Click the check mark to commit the changes.

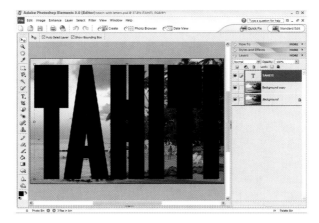

Figure 11.13
Stretch the type using the Move tool.

6. If you want to warp the text, select the Type tool again, click the warp text icon from the options bar, and make your warp choices. (Or with the move tool selected, select Layer > Type > Warp Text.) Click the check mark to commit.

7. Ctrl+click / ⌘+click the Type layer thumbnail in the Layers palette to turn the text into a selection.

8. From the top menu, choose Select > Inverse to reverse the selection.

9. Click the Type layer thumbnail in the Layers palette, and drag it to the Layers palette trashcan. The selection remains on the Background Copy layer, as in Figure 11.14.

Figure 11.14
The reversed selection remains on the Background Copy layer.

10. Click Backspace (Windows) / Delete (Mac) to delete everything around the letters. It will look as though nothing has changed because the original Background layer is still visible.

> **Note:** A gray checkerboard in a layer indicates transparent areas.

11. Click the visibility (eye) icon by the Background layer in the Layers palette to make the Background layer invisible. Only the Background Copy layer will be visible, and the letters will all look cut out, as in Figure 11.15.

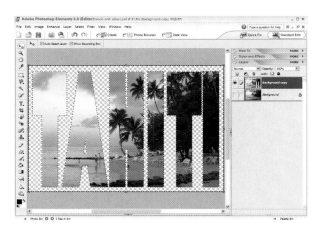

Figure 11.15
The cut-out letters display when the background is invisible.

12. Deselect by pressing Ctrl+D / ⌘+D.

Stylizing the Photo-Filled Text, Option 1

You can make the letters stand out from the background by stylizing them with the layer styles from the Styles and Effects palette.

1. Turn the visibility of the Background layer on by clicking in the layer visibility box next to the Background layer in the Layers palette. The visibility (eye) icon appears.

2. Highlight the Background Copy layer, the one with the letters in it, by clicking it in the Layers palette.

3. In the Styles and Effects palette, choose Layer Styles on the left pull-down menu and any of the styles from the right pull-down menu. Try using a Low drop shadow and a Simple Emboss, as in Figure 11.16.

Figure 11.16
The styled text really stands out on the photograph.

Stylizing the Photo-Filled Text, Option 2

You can stylize the "cut-out" letters on a white or colored background. Print the image, and cut the letters with scissors to paste them on your scrapbook page.

1. Click the Background layer in the Layers palette to highlight the layer.

2. In the top menu, select Edit > Fill Layer.

3. In the Fill Layer dialog box, choose white or a color from the Use pull-down menu.

4. The photo letters will appear against a white or colored Background layer.

5. Click the Background Copy layer in the Layers palette to highlight it.

6. In the Styles and Effects palette, choose Layer Styles on the left pull-down menu and any of the styles from the right pull-down menu. Try using a Soft Edge drop shadow, as in Figure 11.17.

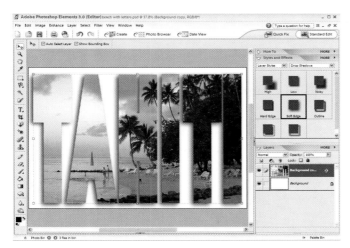

Figure 11.17
Drop-shadowed photo text on a white background

7. Select Layer > Flatten Image before choosing File > Save As to save the file with a new name.

> **Note:** Flatten Image combines all the layers into one final document and creates a smaller file. If you want the option of changing the styles or design later, save the file without flattening the image.

One Last Thought...

Use type creatively. Fonts can convey concepts as easily as images and a stylized word or title can help set the mood for the page. You'll want to experiment with all the options, and Photoshop Elements remembers most steps, so you can undo them and start again. However, applying styles, changing, and undoing require a lot of computer resources. The only limits to the creative possibilities with Photoshop Elements are your imagination, time, and memory—your computer's memory and yours.

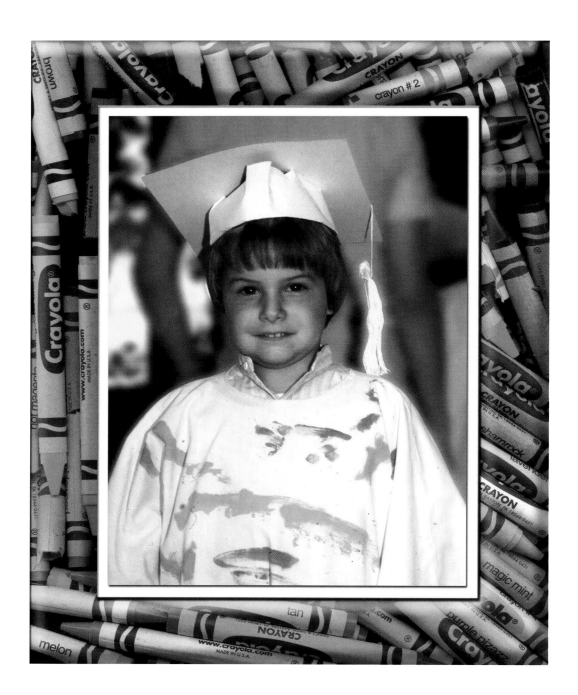

Clip Art
and Backgrounds

Photoshop Elements allows you to create every part of your scrapbook page from scratch. However, Elements also makes it easy to use predesigned clip art and backgrounds available from many sources. In this chapter we'll show how to use predesigned art for your scrapbooks and then how to create originals by using the painting tools in Photoshop Elements. Finally, we'll scan items to create original backgrounds for your projects.

12

Chapter Contents
Using clip art collections
Creating backgrounds
Scanning backgrounds

Using Clip Art Collections

Unlike fonts, you don't have to install clip art and backgrounds onto your hard drive. Insert a CD, such as one from Claudia's Clip Art (www.claudiasclipart.com) or Creating Keepsakes (www.creatingkeepsakes.com), in your computer and browse through the collections using either the Organizer (Windows only) or the File Browser in Photoshop Elements. A PhotoSpin.com subscription allows you to browse extensive collections directly on the Web and download images into any folder you create on your hard drive.

Note: The PhotoSpin.com subscription service offers a large collection of woodcuts, borders, illustrations, textures, and more. The most affordable subscription includes small "presenter-JPG (640×480)" files, which are perfect for embellishments, tags, and borders in scrapbooks. And you can resize these images using the technique on the "Resizing Images to Optimal Print Resolution" recipe card.

We're using the File Browser and the Standard Edit mode for the projects in this chapter. Make it a habit to always save the clip art you modify by going to File > Save As and saving with a new name in a Scrapbook Items folder you create for your project.

Selecting Clip Art

You can use Photoshop Elements to open a clip art file directly from a CD or copy the file first to your hard drive and then open it. Start Photoshop Elements in the Edit and Enhance Photos mode.

1. Select File > Browse Folders.
2. Navigate to the CD or to your Scrapbook Items folder in the Folders tab.
3. Click an image. You'll see the size and resolution of the file in the Metadata tab and a larger preview in the Preview tab, as in Figure 12.1.

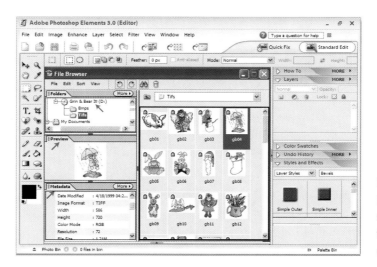

Figure 12.1

Using the File Browser to search through a CD or a folder of downloaded clip art

4. Double-click the image to open it and make sure it has a resolution of 300 pixels/inch at the size you need for your page. See Chapter 9 for image-resizing guidelines, or use the "Resizing Images to Optimal Print Resolution" recipe card.

Changing Colors

Changing the colors of clip art to match the design of your scrapbook page is one of the advantages of creating page parts with Photoshop Elements.

1. Make a selection of one colored area using any selection method. The Magic Wand tool often works well for clip art color selections.

2. Select Edit > Fill Selection.

3. In the Fill Layer dialog box, choose Use and choose a fill color or pattern. Click OK.

You may prefer to apply a gradient to a selected area by selecting the Gradient Tool and dragging across the selection. See Creating Gradients later in this chapter. Figure 12.2 shows several examples.

Figure 12.2
Clip art with its original colors and the changed versions

Creating Backgrounds

Clip art collections often include full-page backgrounds ready for resizing and printing or for building your digital scrapbook page. You can also create your own backgrounds using Photoshop Elements. The following sections contain a few suggestions.

Creating Repetitive Patterns

Use a piece of clip art, a specially designed letter, or any shape you created, and place it repeatedly around a page to use as a scrapbook background.

Clip art JPGs and TIFFs generally appear on one layer with a white background. To use just the clip art, you need to remove the white background. This technique should work with most clip art.

1. Select File > Open, and open the clip art or a special shape and resize it..

2. Double-click the Background layer in the Layers palette, and change the layer name to Layer 0. Click OK.

3. Select the Magic Wand tool, and click an area of the white background to select it.

4. Press Backspace/Delete to remove the white background area.

5. Ctrl+D / ⌘+D to deselect everything. See Figure 12.3.

Figure 12.3

Remove the white background from clip art before you use it to build a digital page.

Build the scrapbook page by dragging and duplicating the clip art.

1. Go to File > New > Blank File to create a document at the size of your scrapbook page. Set the Resolution to 300 pixels/inch and the Color Mode to RGB Color.

Note: Hold the Shift key down as you change the size of any selected item to maintain the proportions of the original.

2. Rotate the clip art by hovering with the Move tool just outside the anchor points. The Move arrow turns into a double-headed arrow. Click and drag to rotate the clip art. Click the check mark in the options bar to commit the move.

3. Repeat steps 3–5 as many times as you want. You'll end up with many layers, as in Figure 12.4.

4. Choose a different page color by clicking the Background layer in the Layers palette and selecting Edit > Fill Layer.

5. Choose a color from the pull down menu in the Fill Layer dialog box, and click OK. See Figure 12.5.

6. Select Layer > Flatten Image to combine all the different layers before saving.

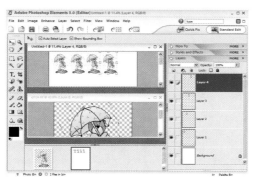 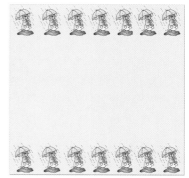

Figure 12.3 Duplicate clip art to make a unique background.   **Figure 12.4** Rainy day background page

Creating Digital Textures

Fill a page with a digital texture from a clip art collection, or create your own.

1. Select File > New > Blank File to create a document the size of your scrapbook page. Set the resolution to 300 pixels/inch. Set the Color Mode option to RGB Color. Leave the Background Contents option set to White for now.

2. In the Styles and Effects palette, select Effects from the left pull-down menu and Textures from the right pull-down menu.

3. Choose a texture, and double-click it to apply it, as in Figure 12.6.

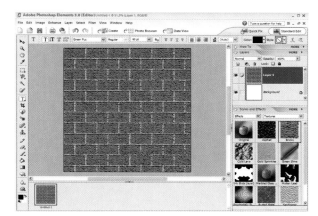

Figure 12.6
Bricks texture

> **Note:** Photoshop Elements can create a variety of textures for a page, but this isn't an instantaneous change. The speed of your computer determines how quickly the effect is applied.

4. Select Layer > Flatten Image to combine all the different layers before saving.

Creating Gradients

You can fill a page with any type of gradient using any color combinations you choose.

1. Select File > New > Blank File to create a document the size of your scrapbook page. Set the resolution to 300 pixels/inch. Set the Color Mode option to RGB Color. Leave the Background Contents option as White for now.

2. Select the Gradient tool, and pick a gradient from the options bar. Use the Edit button to see more presets or design your own. Click OK to close the Gradient Editor dialog box.

> **Tip:** Two of the default gradients are called Foreground to Background and Foreground to Transparent. By choosing your foreground and background colors in the toolbox, you can design your own color gradient.

3. Select a gradient style from one of the five choices in the options bar.

4. Use the Gradient tool to click and drag across your page. Click at any angle, and start from anywhere you choose. The resulting gradient will differ according to the angle and the length of your drag. See Figure 12.7.

5. Select File > Save As, and save the gradient background.

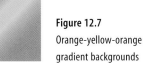

Figure 12.7
Orange-yellow-orange
gradient backgrounds

Scanning Backgrounds

You can scan just about anything and turn it into a background or an embellishment for a scrapbook using Photoshop Elements.

Scanning Items for a Letter-Sized Background

In this section you'll make a background of crayons for a letter size scrapbook page.

1. Cover the scanner glass with a clean piece of plastic wrap, stretching the plastic wrap beyond the edges of the glass. This will prevent the crayons from accidentally coloring the scanner glass and will make removing them easier.

2. Spread the crayons randomly on the plastic wrap–covered scanner glass.

3. Close the scanner lid lightly, and then cover the whole scanner with a black or dark cloth to keep out any external light.

4. Select File > Import, and pick your scanner's name from the pull-down menu.

5. Click Preview or Prescan to see the image as the scanner sees it. Rearrange the crayons if necessary.

Note: Some scanners will automatically start a preview scan, and others will open a controls window. Generally, you should scan every background for scrapbooking with the same settings as a color photo at 300 ppi.

6. If you have a scanning controls window, you should be able to select the following:

   Original: Choose Photo

   Scan Type: Choose Color (True Color)

   Purpose or Destination: Choose Printer

   Resolution: 300 ppi or dpi depending on the scanner

7. If you have a choice for scale or target size, choose 100% or enter a letter-sized page's dimensions. Most scanner beds are at least letter size. Figure 12.8 shows one example of a scanning controls window. Your scanner window may look different, but the selection choices should be similar.

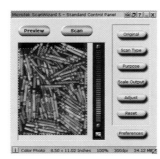

Figure 12.8
Crayon scanning set up using
Microtek's Standard Control Panel

Note: Most scanners allow you to move and resize the "marching ants" selection area by clicking and dragging on the lines.

8. Click the scan button in the scanner controls window on the screen. The scanner will scan the items on the scanner glass.

9. Close the scanner controls window if necessary.

10. The image should now be visible in Photoshop Elements, as in Figure 12.9.

11. If you need to improve the color, select Enhance and choose one of the Auto choices in the top menu. Try them all to see which works best. You can always undo your changes by clicking the blue Undo arrow.

12. Select File > Save As, and save the letter-sized background.

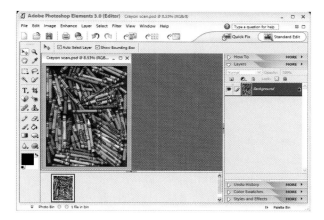

Figure 12.9
A scanned letter-sized page filled with crayons

Changing the Scanned Background to Fit a 12×12 Page

You can crop the newly scanned background to use it for a 12×12 scrapbook. The crayons or other items will be larger, but the 12×12 page will be filled with color.

1. Select the Crop tool in the toolbox.

2. In the options bar, set both the width and height at 12 inches. Set the resolution at 300 pixels/inch.

3. Drag as large an area as possible in the image, as in Figure 12.10.

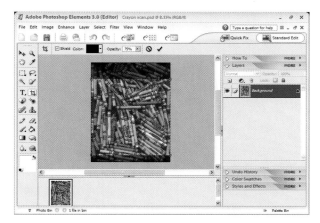

Figure 12.10
Crop the crayon background for a 12×12 scrapbook page.

4. Click the check mark to commit the crop.

5. Select File > Save As, and save the 12×12 background.

Using the Scan as a Frame

You can transform any digital file into a photo frame using Photoshop Elements. Print the frame and cut it out for use in a traditional scrapbook, or use this technique to place a digital photo in the frame and then print both together.

1. Select File > Browse folders, and navigate to the photograph. Double-click to open the file.

2. Select Image > Resize > Image Size. Make sure the photo has a resolution of 300 ppi and has the width and height you want for your page. Resize the photo if necessary using the "Resizing Images to Optimal Print Resolution" recipe card.

3. Select File > Browse folders, and navigate to the background for the frame. Double-click to open the file.

4. Select Image > Resize > Image Size. Make sure the background frame has a resolution of 300 ppi and a width and height about 2 inches larger than your photo. Resize it if necessary using the "Resizing Images to Optimal Print Resolution" recipe card.

5. Click the Tile Windows icon, the four little squares in the right side of the menu bar, to show both the frame and the photo on the screen at the same time.

6. Use the Move tool to click the photo and drag it on top of the frame. The photo will now be on a layer above the background layer, as in Figure 12.12.

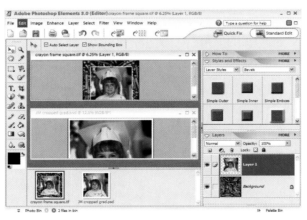

Figure 12.12 Tile the open images, and click-drag the photo onto the frame.

Figure 12.13 Modifying a layer style setting

7. Click the Maximize icon, the small box at the right side of the menu bar, to make the frame and photo image fill the screen.

8. While holding down the Shift key, use the Move tool on the square corner anchors to fit the photo in the frame.

9. Use the Move tool to center the photo in the frame.

Create the look of a 3D frame using the Styles and Effects palette. Choose Layer Styles on the left pull-down menu and Bevels on the right pull-down menu.

1. With Layer 1, the photo layer, highlighted, click Simple Sharp Pillow Emboss in the Layer Styles Bevels choices.

CHAPTER 12: CLIPART AND BACKGROUNDS ■

2. Select Layer > Layer Style > Style Settings. In the Style Settings dialog box, change the bevel direction to Down, as in Figure 12.13. Click OK.

3. Click the Background frame layer in the Layers palette to select it.

4. Click a bevel style to give a 3D look to the frame. Since styles can only be applied to a layer, Elements will ask you if you want to make this background a layer. Click OK, and rename the layer in the New Layer dialog box. Click OK again. Figure 12.14 shows the framed photo.

Figure 12.14
Using the scanned
crayons as a photo frame

Other Ideas

Try some of the following ideas to create a variety of different digital backgrounds to fit any scrapbook page.

- Scan a slightly crumpled piece of tan sandpaper and some shells to make a beach background. Be sure to cover the scanner glass with clear plastic wrap. Put the shells downs first, and lay the sandpaper over them. Remember, the scanner is taking a picture of what it sees on the glass from underneath the glass.

- Place crumpled pieces of cellophane on the scanner glass, and cover these with a piece of colored paper and scan.

- Cover the scanner bed with plastic wrap, and then cover the area with candy corn for a Halloween background.

- Scan the pocket from an old pair of blue jeans for a western background.

- Scan lace or a doily covered with a piece of colored paper or cloth.

- Scan a ski trail map for a skiing page.

- Scan a road map or a country map for a vacation page.

- Scan buttons, medals, ribbons, flowers, labels, or any memorabilia.

- Apply a white or colored layer over a background and fade the layer's opacity for a different effect.

One Last Thought…

Whether you use clip art and predesigned backgrounds or make your own, building parts of a scrapbook page with Photoshop Elements makes customizing easy. Change clip art to fit your design or your imagination. Make a textured background, and use it as a theme for multiple pages. Create original backgrounds from scanned items. Every scrapbook page you design with Photoshop Elements will have a unique look.

Real dolls...
Grow up

Nathalie

The Full Page

Combining traditional paper crafting with digital technology allows you to archive and share your memories in new ways. Once a page is in digital format, you can print it yourself or send it to be printed on a wide-format printer. You may choose to reduce the page and print it on a letter-sized printer as an 8×8-inch version of the page, creating mini–memory books for gifts. You can also burn the file of any page created on the computer or any scanned page to CD or DVD media as an additional archiving method.

13

Chapter Contents

Scanning a photograph, slide, or negative
Printing a photo or other image
Building a digital page
Scanning a 12×12 page with a letter-sized scanner
Printing a scrapbook page

Scanning a Photograph, Slide, or Negative

 Although many newer scanners offer one-button scanning, you'll get better final images for scrapbooks using Photoshop Elements to control the scan.

Scanning a Photograph

Set up your scanner, and install the latest driver according to the manufacturer's directions. Clean the scanner glass, turn on the scanner, and launch Photoshop Elements in the Edit and Enhance Photos mode. The following settings are general guidelines since each scanner has a slightly different interface.

1. Dust off the photo carefully with a bulb blower.
2. Place the photo face down on the scanner glass, lining it up with the sides of the scanner.
3. In Photoshop Elements, select File > Import and choose the scanner by its name or software designation.

 Note: Scan all photos in color (RGB) even if they're black-and-white photos. The scanner will capture more data, making the digital file easier to correct and giving the finished photo a better tonal range.

4. Set your particular scanner's settings to indicate what you're scanning, as in Figure 13.1 or generally as follows:

   Original: Choose Photo (or Reflective on some scanners).

   Scan Type: Choose Color (True Color or RGB on some scanners).

   Resolution or Purpose or Destination: Choose Printer or 300 ppi or dpi depending on the scanner.

   Scale or Target Size: Choose 100% (original), or choose the size you want the image to be for your scrapbook, such as 4×6 or 5×7.

Note: If you plan to use the photo at a larger size than the original, increase the target size. The finished scan should be 300 pixels/inch at the final target size.

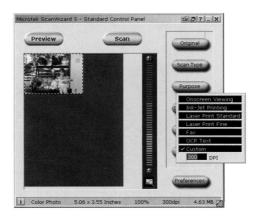

Figure 13.1
Microtek ScanWizard settings for scanning a photograph

5. Click Preview or Prescan to see your photo as the scanner sees it.

6. Move the selection area by clicking and dragging the selection lines to match your photo or the area of the photo you want to capture.

7. Click Scan to scan the image. When the scanner finishes the scan, close the scanner window if necessary or just return to Photoshop Elements.

8. Your photo should now be in the Photoshop Elements window as an untitled file. Select File > Save As, and give the scanned image file a name.

> **N o t e :** Scan tags, medals, documents, ribbons, and other memorabilia for your scrapbooks using the settings for a photograph.

Scanning a Slide or Negative

You need a flatbed scanner with a transparency adapter (or a dedicated film scanner) to scan slides and negatives. Follow the scanner manufacturer's setup guide for the adapter, turn on the scanner, and launch Photoshop Elements in the Edit and Enhance Photos mode.

1. Dust off the slide or negative carefully with a bulb blower.

2. Place the slide or negative in the slide or film holder provided by the scanner manufacturer. For most flatbed scanners, place the slide or negative such that the "front" is face down on the scanner glass. (Scanner instructions generally say "emulsion side up," but it's sometimes difficult to see the emulsion on the film.) To determine the front of the slide or negative, hold it up to a light so that the image looks like the printed photo should look. The side facing you will be the "front."

> **N o t e :** Hold the slide or negative to a light so you can see the image as if it were a photograph; in other words, hold it so that it looks like the photo should look. Put the slide or negative with the front side facing down on the glass.

3. Remove the document mat, if your scanner has one, from the underside of the scanner lid to reveal a translucent strip or another light source. To scan a slide or negative, the light has to go through the transparent slide or negative.

4. In Photoshop Elements, select File > Import and choose your scanner or scanner wizard.

> **N o t e :** You may need to select a different scanning mode, such as Standard, Home, or Professional to see the choices for slides and negatives.

5.   Indicate what you're scanning in the scanner settings dialog box. Scanner settings will vary depending on the brand and model. Use settings closest in meaning to the following ones:

Original or Document Type: Choose Transparency and either Slide (Film Positive) or Negative (Film Negative on some scanners). Figure 13.2 shows the choices available for document types on an Epson scanner in the Home mode.

Scan or Image Type: Choose Color (True Color or RGB on some scanners).

Resolution or Purpose or Destination: Choose Printer or 300 ppi or dpi. The final image resolution for scrapbook images should be 300 pixels/inch at the final image size. A slide or negative is generally much smaller than the final print. Most scanners automatically make the calculations if you set the desired size and image resolution. If your scanner doesn't, you'll need to determine a higher resolution for scanning. As a guide, choose 1200 for scanning resolution to scan a 35mm slide or negative for a final 4×6 inch photo or 1500 for a 5×7.

Scale or Target Size: Choose the size you want the image to be for your scrapbook, such as 4×6 or 5×7.

Figure 13.2
Original or document types

6.   Click Preview to see the image as the scanner sees it. Figure 13.3 shows a preview of a slide scan and the appropriate settings to create a 4×6 image for printing.

Figure 13.3
Slide scanning set up with an Epson Stylus Photo RX500

7.   Move the selection area if needed to match your slide or negative.

8. Click Scan to scan the image. When the scanner has finished, close the scanner software window if necessary and return to Photoshop Elements.

9. Your slide or negative should now be in the Elements window as an untitled file. Select File > Save As, and give the scanned image file a name.

Printing a Photo or Other Image

Once you've scanned a photo, negative, or slide, you'll want to "fix" it in Photoshop Elements. Make any enhancements in either the Quick Fix mode or the Standard Edit mode. You can then save the fixed photo to build a digital page, send the photo to an online printing service, or print it on an ink-jet printer. The ink-jet printer setup is basically the same for printing photographs or scrapbook elements created in Photoshop Elements.

1. Select File > Print. Your image appears in the Print Preview dialog box with the current paper size settings, as in Figure 13.4.

2. Choose Page Setup. In Windows, select Printer from the Page Setup dialog box, and choose Properties to specify individual settings for your printer. On a Mac, select the printer, the paper size, and the orientation from the pull-down menus in the Page Setup dialog box.

3. Set the paper size and type. Select the best photo print quality available. Click OK until you return to the Page Setup dialog box.

4. Make sure the size and orientation are correct for your image. Click OK again to return to the Print Preview dialog box. On a Mac, make sure the Print Size pull-down menu is set to the desired print size in the Print Preview dialog box.

   Your image should appear in the correct orientation and size on the page. See Figure 13.5.

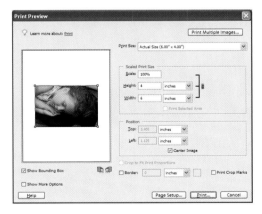

Figure 13.4 Print Preview dialog box before selecting printer and page setup.

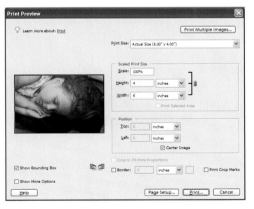

Figure 13.5 Print Preview dialog box with settings for a 4×6 borderless photo

5. Click Print. Photoshop Elements opens a message stating, "Some PostScript specific print settings will be ignored since you are printing to a non-PostScript printer." Click OK. You don't need a PostScript printer to print photos and scrapbook pages with Photoshop Elements.

Building a Digital Page

Whether you cut and paste with scissor and glue or build a digital page, the basic process is the same. Gather all the parts and tools, sketch the layout, and start adding elements to a blank page.

Gathering the Page Parts

With digital scrapbooking, everything is in one place: the computer. Launch Photoshop Elements in the Standard Edit mode, and start with a blank page.

1. Select File > New > Blank File, or click the New file icon in the shortcuts bar.

2. Choose the following page settings:

   Name: The name of the page you're building

   Width and Height: The size of your scrapbook

   Resolution: 300 pixels/inch

   Color Mode: RGB Color

   Background Contents: White

3. Optional: Turn on the rulers or the grid if your page will have a geometric look. Ctrl+R / ⌘+R, or select View > Rulers. Select View > Grid to turn on and off the grid.

4. Select File > Open or File > Browse Folders, and open the photos.

5. Make any final adjustments to the photos using the Enhance menu in the Standard Editor mode, or click Quick Fix to make the changes in the Quick Fix mode.

6. Check the size of each photo. Select Image > Resize > Image Size. All the photos should be at 300 pixels/inch at the width and height for your design. Change the photo sizes if necessary, but maintain the resolution at 300 ppi. (Use the technique in Chapter 9.)

7. Crop the photos to emphasize the important areas using any Photoshop Elements cropping tools.

   All open images should be in the Photo Bin, as in Figure 13.6.

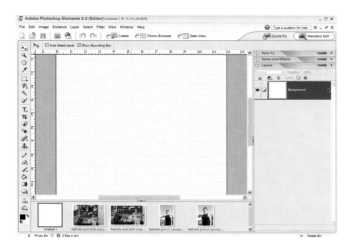

Figure 13.6
The page parts are available
in the Photo Bin.

Creating the Background

You can open a previously designed background, use one from a clip art collection, or make one as you build the page. Perform the following steps to create one style of a "torn fiber" background. Try other shapes and layer filters to design any style you can imagine.

1. Duplicate the Background layer by dragging it over the New Layer icon in the Layers palette.

2. Select Edit > Fill Layer, and choose a color to fill the Background Copy layer.

> **Note:** To choose a color from a photo, use the Eyedropper tool to click a color in an open photo. The color becomes the foreground color in the toolbox.

3. Using the Rectangular Marquee tool, make a selection on the left side of the colored background, as in Figure 13.8.

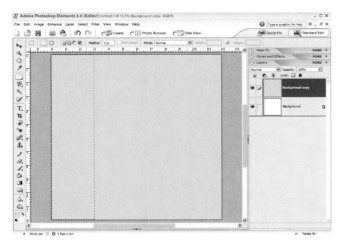

Figure 13.7
Selecting an area on the
Background Copy layer

4. Ctrl+J / ⌘+J to jump the selected rectangle to its own layer. Rename the layer Fiber Border.

Note: You can rename any layer by double-clicking its name in the Layers palette.

5. In the Styles and Effects palette, choose Filters on the left pull-down menu and Texture on the right pull-down menu.

6. Double-click a texture thumbnail, and change the options in the dialog box, as in Figure 13.8. To reset the settings, hold Alt/Option, and the Cancel button changes to a Reset button. Try different settings until the border looks like a fiber border.

7. Click OK to apply the texture to the border layer.

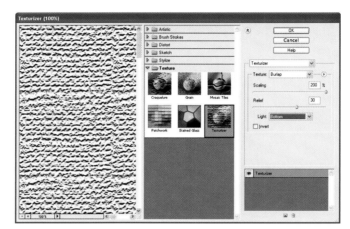

Figure 13.8
The Texturizer dialog box from the Styles and Effects palette

Tip: You can reset most variations dialog boxes in Photoshop Elements to the default settings by holding the Alt/Option key and clicking the Reset (Cancel) button.

8. Select the Rectangular Marquee tool to select a thin vertical area along the edge of the Fiber Border layer to create the torn edge.

9. Ctrl+J / ⌘+J to jump the selected area to its own layer. Rename the layer Torn Edge.

10. In the Styles and Effects palette, choose Filters on the left pull-down menu and Stylize on the right pull-down menu.

11. Double-click a style such as Wind, drag the cursor in the checkerboard to see the edge, and choose variations as in Figure 13.9. Click OK to apply the filter to the edge.

Figure 13.9
The Blast variation of the Wind stylized filter

12. Choose Distort from the right pull-down menu in the Styles and Effects palette, and double-click ZigZag.

13. In the ZigZag dialog box, increase the Ridges slider to 20, and choose Out from Center in the Style pull-down menu.

14. Click OK. The fiber border has a torn edge look, as in Figure 13.10.

Tip: You can lock each of the layers you create to protect them as you build the page. Select each layer, and click the padlock icon in the Layers palette.

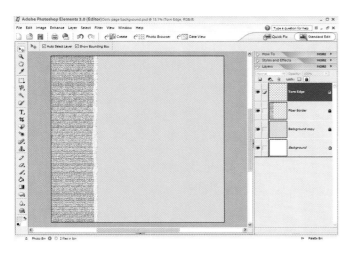

Figure 13.10
A fiber border with a "torn edge". The layers are locked in the Layers palette.

Placing the Photos

Place each of the photos from the Photo Bin onto your background page just as you would in traditional scrapbooking.

1. Make sure the top (Torn Edge) layer is highlighted in the Layers palette.

2. Click the Tile Windows icon in the main menu to see all the images at the same time, as in Figure 13.11.

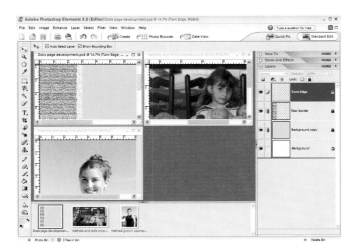

Figure 13.11
All the images are visible in the Photoshop Elements Editor window.

3. Use the Move tool to click and drag each photo onto the background.

4. With the Background layer selected, click the Maximize icon in the top menu. Don't worry if you can't see all your photos. They may be on top of one another.

5. Select the Move tool. Click one photo layer at a time, and move the photos into position.

6. Resize each photo using the Move tool. Hold the Shift key as you click and drag the corner anchor points.

7. Rotate one or more photos using the Move tool by hovering the cursor just outside the selected area. The arrow turns into a double-headed arrow. Click and drag to rotate the image.

Note: Making photos smaller is fine. Enlarging photos by stretching them with the Move tool may make them fuzzy. Use the resizing technique in Chapter 9 before you place the photo on the page.

Adding a Stylized Stroke as a Photo Frame

You can add a frame to the photos and match the frame color to any color in the page.

1. Select the Move tool and click the first photo in the image.

2. Select Edit > Stroke (Outline) Selection. In the Stroke dialog box, pick a large pixel width such as 50 pixels and choose Outside for the location, as in Figure 13.12.

3. Click the color box in the Stroke dialog box and move the Color Picker dialog box out of the way so you can click on a color in your image. The Cursor turns into the Eyedropper tool. Click a color for the border. Click OK in the Color Picker dialog box and OK in the Stroke dialog box to apply the colored stroke.

Figure 13.12
The Stroke dialog box

4. In the Styles and Effects palette, choose Layer Styles on the left pull-down menu and Bevels on the right pull-down menu. Click on a bevel style to apply it.

5. Choose Drop Shadows from the right pull-down menu, and click any drop shadow style to apply it.

Copying Layer Styles to Other Photos

You can copy and reapply layer styles and effects from one layer to another, and all the photos will have the same frame style.

1. With the previous photo layer still highlighted in the Layers palette, select Layer > Layer Style > Copy Layer Style. See Figure 13.13.

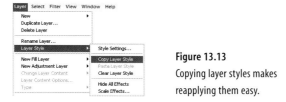

Figure 13.13
Copying layer styles makes reapplying them easy.

2. Use the Move tool and click the next photo in the image.
3. Select Edit > Stroke (Outline) Selection. Apply the same settings as for the other photograph. (The previous settings are already in the Stroke dialog box.) Click OK.
4. Select Layer > Layer Style > Paste Layer Style to apply the same frame style as for the other photo.

Adding Type

Using Photoshop Elements you can easily add stylized page titles and names that match the colors in your design.

1. Set the foreground color to match a color in any image by selecting the Eyedropper tool, changing the sample size in the options bar to 3 by 3 average, and clicking the color in that image.
2. Click the top layer in the Layers palette to highlight it.
3. Select the Horizontal or Vertical Type tool from the toolbox and a font, font style, and size from the options bar, as in Figure 13.14.

Figure 13.14 Using the Type tool and Type options bar

> **Tip:** You can change font, font style, size, and color after typing by selecting the Type tool and clicking the text in the Image.

4. Place the cursor in the page and type. Click the check mark. Enter another area of text, and click the check mark again.
5. Select the Move tool and click the text to reposition it on the page.
6. In the Styles and Effects palette, choose Layer Styles on the left pull-down menu and any of the choices on the right pull-down menu. Click on a bevel style, drop shadow, inner shadow, or any combination to apply the style to one Type layer.
7. Select Layer > Layer Style > Copy Layer Style.
8. Use the Move tool to click another Type layer.
9. Select Layer > Layer Style > Paste Layer Style to apply the same styles as for the first Type layer.

Finishing the Page

To make the photographs and text stand out more, reduce the opacity of the main colored background.

1. Click the Background Copy layer in the Layers palette.
2. Click the padlock icon in the Layers palette to unlock the Background Copy layer.
3. Click the Opacity pull-down at the top of the Layers palette, and use the slider to reduce the opacity, as in Figure 13.15.

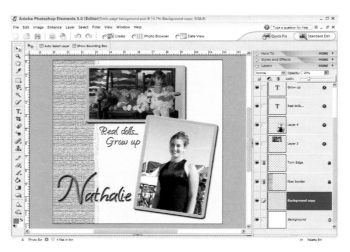

Figure 13.15

Reducing the opacity of the background increases the visibility of the photographs and type.

4. Select File > Save As to save the file with all the layers, or select Layer > Flatten Image and then File > Save As to save the file as one layer.

Scanning a 12×12 Page with a Letter-Sized Scanner

Flatbed scanners with a scanner bed large enough to scan a 12×12 scrapbook page in one pass are large and expensive. Using Photoshop Elements, you can scan a 12×12 page with any letter size or larger flatbed scanner by scanning the four corners separately and then assembling the page. The Photomerge Panorama feature in Elements was designed for photographers who want to merge a series of photographs into a wide panorama. Scrapbookers can use this tool to merge separately scanned page segments.

 Tip: Quit any other applications that may be running. Photoshop Elements will need a large amount of RAM to create the Photomerge.

Scanning the Page

In addition to your scanner, your computer, and the scrapbook page, you'll need two small rulers or straight edges that fit on the scanner glass area and a black cloth large enough to drape over the closed scanner. Using the rulers moves the edges of the page away from the borders of the scanner bed so you can scan the page completely to the edge. The black cloth prevents external light from reaching the scanner "cameras."

Scanning the First Corner

For the best results, set up each segment carefully and align the page with the rulers and the sides of the scanner glass. Start Photoshop Elements in the Standard Edit mode.

1. Dust off the scanner glass with a bulb blower and a clean soft cloth.

2. Align the two rulers to make a corner along the top-left corner of the scanner glass. See Figure 13.16. Some scanners start scanning from the bottom-left corner. It doesn't matter. Just be consistent since you'll repeat this step four times.

Figure 13.16
Line up the two rulers in the top-left corner on the scanner glass.

3. Place the 12×12 page face down on the scanner glass. Align the top-left corner of the page with the rulers in top-left corner of the scanner.

4. Close the scanner lid lightly. The rulers and the page will prevent the scanner from closing completely.

5. Cover the scanner with the black cloth to prevent external light from reaching the scanner.

6. Select File > Import, and choose your scanner.

7. Change the scanner's mode from Auto or Basic to Home or Professional mode, so you can control the size of the scan.

8. Choose the settings as in Figure 13.17. Most scanners will have similar settings.

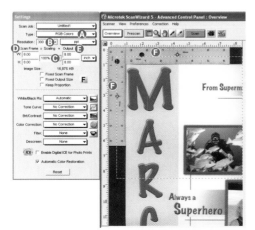

Figure 13.17 Microtek ScanWizard settings for scanning a 12×12 page

Original: Photo (Reflective on some scanners)

Scan Type (A): Color (True Color or RGB on some scanners)

Resolution (B): 300 ppi or dpi

Scale (C): 100%

Original (D): (Scan Frame or Source on some scanners)

W = 8 inches

H = 8 inches

Target (E): (Output on some scanners)

W = 8 inches

H = 8 inches

9. Click Preview or Prescan to see your photo as the scanner sees it.

10. Move the selection area (F) to include a small portion of the rulers, as in Figure 13.17.

Note: Photomerge combines the scans with an overlap. Scanning each side at 8×8 inches leaves just enough overlap for each merge.

11. Click Scan to scan the image. When the scanner finishes the scan, close the scanner window if necessary.

12. The top-left corner of the scrapbook page should now be in Photoshop Elements as an untitled file. Select File > Save As, and name the file TopLft.psd. Save each corner scan in the .psd format.

Tip: If you make any color changes to the scan, be sure to save the settings so can be applied to the next three scans of the page.

Scanning the Other Three Corners

You need to scan the other three corners, maintaining the same settings. If your scanner is legal size, 8½×14, you'll have to scan only the two top corners, not all four.

1. Move the rulers and align them to make a corner along the top-right corner of the scanner glass (the bottom-right on some scanners).

2. Place the 12×12 page face down on the scanner glass, aligning the top-right corner of the 12×12 page with the rulers.

3. Repeat steps 4 through 9 in the previous section. Keep the settings the same as for the previous scan.

4. Move the selection area to match the top-right corner of your scrapbook page.

5. Click Scan. When the scanner finishes, close the scanner window.

6. The top-right corner of the scrapbook page should now be in Photoshop Elements as an untitled file. Select File > Save As, and name the file TopRt.psd.

7. Repeat all the steps two more times.

- Move the rulers, page, and selection area to scan the bottom left of the page. Select File > Save As, and name the file BotLft.psd.

- Move the rulers, page, and scan area to scan the bottom right of the page. Select File > Save As, and name the file BotRt.psd.

Note: Take your time with each corner to set up the page evenly with the rulers. The straighter the scans, the better the merged page.

The last scan appears in the Photoshop Elements window; you should also see four scanned page parts in the Photo Bin, as in Figure 13.18.

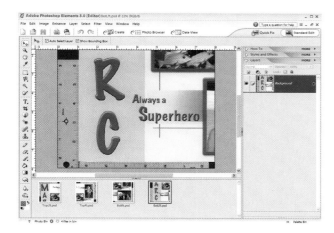

Figure 13.18
Four corner scans

Merging the Four Corner Scans

Photoshop Elements makes merging the four corner scans an easy process.

1. Select File > New > Photomerge Panorama, as in Figure 13.19.
2. The four corner scans should be listed as the source files in the Photomerge dialog box, as in Figure 13.20. You can click Browse to find them if necessary.

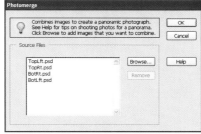

Figure 13.19 Photomerge Panorama pull-down menu

Figure 13.20 Photomerge dialog box

3. Click OK, and watch the Photoshop Elements magic!
4. The next Photomerge dialog box shows a preview of the merge page. See Figure 13.21.

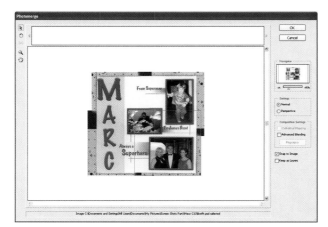

Figure 13.21
Photomerge dialog box
with preview of merge

5. Click OK, and let Photoshop Elements assemble the page. The final merge shows as a new untitled file, as in Figure 13.22.

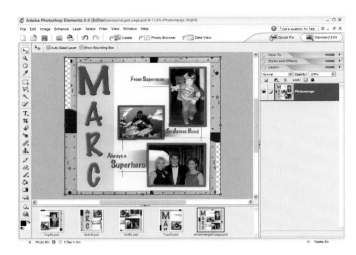

Figure 13.22
Finished Photomerge in Photoshop
Elements window

Note: If Elements merges only two or three of the four corners, the application may need more memory. Quit Photoshop Elements and all other applications. Restart Elements, and open the four images you just scanned. Select File > New > Photomerge Panorama, and try again.

If Photoshop Elements couldn't merge your page parts, the individual files will appear in the light box at the top of the screen. This usually means that Elements couldn't find the overlapping areas to merge. Your scans may not be straight. You can try to manually drag the page parts together in the work area, or you can scan one or more of the corners again. Scanning the corners takes practice. If you line up the four corner scans carefully, Elements will be able to assemble the page for you.

Cropping to Size

The merged image includes parts of the rulers and scanner background. Use the Crop tool to crop the page.

1. Select the Crop tool, set the width and height to 12 inches each, and set the resolution to 300 pixels/inch in the options bar. See Figure 13.23.

Figure 13.23 Setting the Crop tool options

2. Click and drag across the image, starting at the top-left corner of the page.

3. Zoom in using the keyboard command: Ctrl+= / ⌘+=. Use the scroll bars to see each corner.

4. Adjust the crop area by moving the corner anchors in or out until only the scrapbook page is selected. See Figure 13.24.

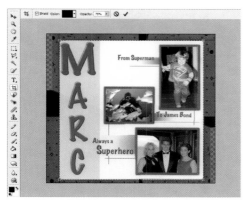

Figure 13.24
Adjusting the cropping area

5. Click the check mark to complete the crop.

The finished scanned page should now look like your paper scrapbook page. If your page has gradations of colors that aren't in the original, the scanner saw external light. See Figure 13.25. Try rescanning the page being careful to cover the entire scanner with a black cloth.

Figure 13.25
Light leaks cause gradations
in the final image.

6. Select File > Save As, and save the merged page.

> **Note:** Scanning page parts and merging works well with many scrapbook pages. However, scanning pages with high 3D items can create shadows when you scan and many gradations when you merge. Use a digital camera on a tripod to photograph such pages or scan them with a professional tabloid-sized scanner.

Printing a Scrapbook Page

If you have an ink-jet photo printer that can use 13×19-inch paper, called Super B or Super A3 size, print your pages on the large paper and then trim the printed page to 12×12 inches. You can also send the file to an online service for large photo prints.

> **Note:** Currently no ink-jet printers can print on 12×12 paper without leaving white margins.

If you have a letter-sized ink-jet photo printer, you can print "mini" 8×8-inch scrapbook pages for gift books.

1. Select File > Print.

2. In the Print Preview dialog box, change the height and width in the Scaled Print Size area to 8 inches each. See Figure 13.26.

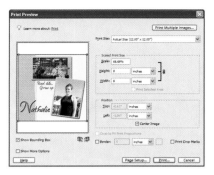

Figure 13.26

Preparing to print a
12×12 page for an 8×8
mini scrapbook album,
using the Print Preview
dialog box.

3. Click Page Setup, verify your printer settings, set the paper type, and click OK to return to the Print Preview dialog box.

4. Click Print.

One Last Thought...

Don't give up the scissors and glue. Digital scrapbooking just adds new tools and many more design options. Use the best of both worlds: combine traditional scrapbooking methods and scrapbooking with Photoshop Elements. You'll save time and money and bring your creativity to a whole new level. With Photoshop Elements you can draw and paint without being an artist, become a better photographer by enhancing your everyday snapshots, and transform photos into memorable page elements. We've merely explored some of the many tools in Photoshop Elements and described a selection of digital scrapbooking recipes. The projects in this creative cropping cookbook are only the beginning. You can design anything you can imagine. The creative possibilities using Photoshop Elements are endless.

N o t e : Exploring all the features of Photoshop Elements requires a separate book, such as *Photoshop Elements 3 Solutions* by Mikkel Aaland (Sybex, 2004). Mikkel describes Photoshop Elements from a photographer's perspective.

Appendix: Easy Monitor Calibration with a Colorimeter

Whether you're trying to fix a photograph or design parts of a scrapbook page, you want the color you see to be as consistent as possible. And since you're judging your images by what you see on the monitor, the way your monitor displays color is very important. Using a colorimeter is the easiest and most accurate way to calibrate a monitor. This appendix shows you how.

Getting Your Monitor in Sync

Although many monitors have adjustment dials, turning them makes changes only to suit your view. The actual color information in the digital image may be different. And as a monitor ages, it changes in brightness and color. An LCD retains its color fidelity longer, but a CRT is considered old after three years.

Note: A colorimeter can be a worthwhile investment, not only helping you see the color of your work more accurately but also adding a little more life to an older monitor.

The only way to accurately adjust the color on any monitor, even revive an older one, is to use *profiling* software and a hardware *colorimeter*. Profiling software analyzes the colors recorded by the colorimeter attached to your computer and creates a *profile*, a data file describing how this particular monitor shows colors. The video card inside your computer then uses the new profile to compensate for your monitor and to display the color according to an International Color Consortium (ICC) standard. Although the explanation sounds complicated, using a colorimeter and its software is extremely easy. The two manufacturers of calibration tools used most by professional photographers and designers, GretagMacbeth and Monaco by X-Rite, also make more affordable versions called the GretagMacbeth Eye-One Display and the MonacoOPTIX^{XR} (see Figure A.1).

Figure A.1 The GretagMacbeth Eye-One Display (left) and Monaco OPTIX^XR (right)

Calibrating and Profiling

Colorimeters work the same way on both Windows and Macintosh. Follow these steps for calibrating with GretagMacbeth's Eye-One Display (Using the MonacoOPTIX^XR is very similar):

1. Clean the monitor screen with a soft cloth. Never spray any cleaning liquids on your monitor.

2. Turn on the computer. For a CRT, let the monitor warm up for 30 minutes. LCDs don't require warm-up time.

3. Turn all adjustment dials on the monitor to the midpoint position.

4. Install the profiling software from the CD on your computer.

5. Plug the colorimeter cable into a USB port on your computer.

6. Launch the Eye-One Match software. Click the monitor image and follow the step-by-step instructions on the screen. Click the forward arrow after each step. You can click the arrows in the Help Column for detailed explanations. See Figure A.2.

Figure A.2
Eye-One Display interface and help menu

7. Choose the Easy or Advanced mode and indicate whether you have a CRT or LCD.

   Easy mode lets the software determine the *white point* and *gamma* according to what type of monitor and computer it senses.

   Advanced mode allows you to choose the *white point* and *gamma*.

White Point and Gamma

White point defines the "color" of white on your monitor. Generally, 6500° Kelvin is considered daylight and is a good setting for monitor calibration. As a guide, 5000° Kelvin is somewhat yellow or warm, and 9300° Kelvin is bluer or cool.

Gamma refers to the relationship between the pixels in your computer and the way the monitor shows light. Usually 2.2 is normal for a PC and 1.8 is normal for a Mac.

8. Put the colorimeter on any matte black surface and click Calibrate. When the software indicates the colorimeter is calibrated, click the arrow to continue.

9. Now place the colorimeter on the monitor screen.

> CRT: Push the colorimeter lightly so the suction cups grip the glass.

> LCD: Gently place the colorimeter on the screen, and hang the counterweight on the cable over the top of the monitor to keep it in place.

10. Click the right arrow to continue. Colored boxes will appear and disappear on your screen as the software locates the colorimeter and measures the colors. It beeps when it's done.

11. The software names and dates the profile. Click the right arrow to save the profile in the system. Click OK to finish.

12. Quit the Eye-One Match software application, and unplug the device.

Tip: Calibrate and profile on a regular schedule: monthly if your monitor is fairly new or weekly if it's getting old.

Index

Note to the Reader: Throughout this index **boldfaced** page numbers indicate primary discussions of a topic. *Italicized* page numbers indicate illustrations.

A

absolute positioning in tablets, 70, *71*
achromatic color, 13
active tablet areas, 70–71
AD (analog to digital) converters, **29**
adjustment layers, 93
Adobe Gamma, 73
Advanced calibration node, 169
alignment
    ink-jet print heads, 62
    on pages, **21–23**, *21–23*
    scanner images, 49
all-in-one scanners, 43, *43*
Amount setting for sharpening, 105–106
analog to digital (AD) converters, **29**
anti-aliasing, 128
archiving digital files, **76–79**, *77–79*
artistic effects, **117–121**, *117–121*
asymmetrical balance, 2, *2*
attributes, text, 128
Auto Color option, 97
Auto Contrast option, 97
Auto Fix feature, **88**, *88*
Auto Levels option, 97
automatic mode in digital cameras, 34

B

Background Contents option for clip art, 142–143
backgrounds
    clip art for, **141–142**, *142*
    opacity of, 160, *160*
    for pages, **155–157**, *155–157*
    scanning, **144–147**, *144–147*
    in text, **134–137**, *134–137*
backups
    CDs for, **82–83**, *83*
    contact sheets for, **83–85**, *84–85*
balance, rule of, **2–3**, *2–3*
batteries
    for digital cameras, **34**, 37
    in UPSs, 79
Belkin UPSs, 79, *79*
bit-depth of scanners, **43**, *44*
bitmapped images, 131–132
black-and-white photos
    from color, **98–99**, *98–99*
    colorizing, **121–122**, *122*
blackouts, 79
blemishes, retouching, **104**, *105*
Blending mode for layers, 93
blocks, aligning, 23, *23*
brownouts, 79
Brush tool, 122
Brush Selection tool, 120
built-in memory card slots, **60**

C

cables
    for ink-jet printers, 63
    for scanners, 45, *45*
calibrating monitors, 49, **72–74**, **168–170**, *169*
cameras. *See* digital cameras
Canon Digital Rebel cameras, 28, *28*
Canon i900 printers, 60, *60*
Canon PowerShot cameras, 28, *28*, 32, 35, *35*
Canvas Size dialog box, 115
capital letters, 17, *17*
capture speeds for digital cameras, 35
card readers, **38–39**, *39*
cartridge types, 58, *58*
cathode ray tubes (CRTs), 73
CCDs (charged coupled devices), 29
CDs
    for archives, **77–78**
    for backups, **82–83**, *83*
    printing to, 60
center aligned text, 21, *21*
charged coupled devices (CCDs), 29
charging batteries, 37
Claudia's Clip Art, 140
cleaning
    ink-jet heads, **64–65**, *65*
    scanner glass, 49, 52
Clear Layer Style option, 117
clip art, **139**
    for backgrounds, **141–142**, *142*
    collections of, **140**
    color for, **141–143**, *141*
    digital textures for, **142–143**, *143*
    gradients for, 141, **143**, *143*
    selecting, **140–141**, *140*
CMOS (complementary metal oxide semiconductor) sensors, 29
CMYK color in printing, 56–58
collections in Organizer, 85
color
    for clip art, **141–143**, *141*
    for frames, **114–115**
    hue, lightness, and saturation, **13–14**
    for ink-jet printers, 58, *58*
    in monitors, 73
    for prints, 75
    for text letters, **132–133**
    wise use of, **14–15**, *15*
color gamut, 75
color laser printers, 57
Color Mode option, 142–143
color photos, black-and-white photos from, **98–99**, *98–99*
Color Picker dialog box
    for clip art, 141
    for text letters, 132
color wheel, 13, *13*
colorimeters, 73, **168–170**, *169*
colorizing black-and-white photos, **121–122**, *122*
complementary colors, 13
complementary metal oxide semiconductor (CMOS) sensors, 29

compression in digital cameras, **31–32**
connections
    cameras to computers, 38
    scanners to computers, **45–48**, *45*, *47*
consistency, repetition for, 24
Contact Sheet II dialog box, 85, *85*
contact sheets, **83–85**, *84–85*
Contrast, **23–25**, *25*
contrast ratio in monitors, 73
Cookie Cutter tool
    for cropping, **108–109**, *108–109*
    for frames, 115–116
    for punch shapes, 109
cool hues, 13
Copy Layer Style option, 159
copying
    layer styles, **158–159**
    shapes, **110**, *110*
Creating Keepsakes site, 140
cropping and Crop tool, 99, **106–107**
    Cookie Cutter for, **108–109**, *108–109*
    Marquee tool for, **107**, *108*
    for merged images, **164–165**, *164–165*
    quick, **99**, *99*
    for scanned backgrounds, 145
    for sports trading cards, 124
    in Standard Edit mode, **106–107**
CRTs (cathode ray tubes), 73

D

da Vinci, Leonardo, 4, *4*
darkness, 12
decorative typefaces, 16, *16*
deleting layers, 93
depth for frames, **116–117**, *116*
design, **9**, **19**
    alignment, **21–23**, *21–23*
    color, **13–15**, *13–15*
    contrast, **24–25**, *25*
    lines, **10**, *10*
    mass, **10–11**, *11*
    page rules, **1**
        Rule of Balance, **2–3**, *2–3*
        Rule of Negative Space, **6**, *7*
        Rule of Thirds, **5–6**, *5–6*
        Rule of Visual Center, **3–4**, *4*
    proximity in, **20**, *20*
    repetition, **24**, *24*
    shapes, **10**, *10*
    texture, **11–12**, *12*
    type, **15–17**, *17*
    value, **12**, *12*
digital cameras, 27
    AD converters in, 29
    batteries for, 34
    flash in, 33
    image sensors in, 29
    lenses in, 29–30
    maintaining, **37–38**
    memory cards for, **33–34**, *33*
    pixels in, 28
    resolution and compression in, **31–32**
    retrieving pictures from, **38–39**
    setting up, **38**
    settings for, **34–36**, *35–36*
    shopping list, 37
    shutter-release buttons in, **32**
    types of, **28**, *28*
    viewfinders in, 32
    zoom in, **30–31**, *30–31*

digital SLR (single lens reflex) cameras, 28, *28*
digital textures, **142–143**, *143*
digital zoom, **30–31**, *30–31*
digitizing tablets, **70–72**, *70–72*
direct printing from digital cameras, **60**
Display Calibrator Assistant, 73
display conditions for prints, 74
DMax scanners, **44**
dot-matrix printers, 57
dot pitch in monitors, 73
dpi (dots per inch)
    for ink-jet printers, **57–58**
    for scanners, 44, 48
drivers
    for ink-jet printers, 62, *63*
    for scanners, **46**
Drop Shadows option
    for mosaic photo effect, 123
    for sports trading cards, 125
droplet size in ink-jet printers, **57–58**
drum scanners, 42
Dry Media Brushes option, 120, *120*
DuoSwitch buttons, 72
duplex printing, 61
dust in ink-jet printers, 64
DVDs
    for archives, **77–78**
    printing to, 60
dye sublimation printers, 57
dyes for prints, 75

E

Easy mode in calibration, 169
Edit and Enhance Photos mode, 87, 150
editable text, stylizing, **128–130**, *128–130*
editing tools, **88–93**
Editor for photo fixing, **87–88**, *87*
effects, **95**, **113**
    artistic, **117–121**, *117–121*
    colorizing black-and-white photos, **121–122**, *122*
    cropping, **99**, *99*
    enhancements, **97–98**
    frames and mattes, **113–117**, *113–116*
    layer styles for, **111**, *111*
    mosaic photo effect, **122–123**, *123*
    Quick Fix mode, **96**
    red-eye correction, **96–97**, *96–97*
    retouching, **101–106**, *102–106*
    sepia tone photos from color, **98–99**, *98–99*
    sports trading cards, **124–125**, *124–125*
    text, **127**
        backgrounds and photos in text, **134–137**, *134–137*
        painting text, **131–133**, *132–133*
        stylizing editable text, **128–130**, *128–130*
        text in photographs, **130–131**, *130–131*
Elliptical Marquee tool
    for cropping, 107
    for frames, 114
emotion, reflecting, 23, *23*
enhancements, **97–98**
Epson products
    ink, 75–76
    printers, **59–60**, *59–60*
    scanners, 43, *43*
ergonomics in digital cameras, 36
external hard drives, **76–77**, *77*
Eye-One Display, 73, **168–169**, *169*
Eyedropper tool
    for frames, 114–115
    for sports trading cards, 124

F

feathering selections, 102
feedback in digital cameras, 32
File Browser for clip art, 140, *140*
file size of scanner images, **51**
files, organizing, **85–87**, *86–87*
fill layers and filling
    for backgrounds, 155
    for clip art, 141–142
    for cropping, 107
    for painted drawings, 119
    for shapes, 110
    for text
        with backgrounds and photos, **134–137**, *134–137*
        letters, **132–133**
film scanners, 42, *42*
filters. *See* effects
Find Edges option, 118
Firewire cables, 45, *45*
flash drives, **76**
flash in digital cameras, **33**
Flash memory cards, 33
flat-panel displays, 73
flat-screen monitors, 73
flatbed scanners, 42, *43*
Flatten All Layers option, 85
Flatten Image option
    for clip art, 142–143
    for frames, 114
    for painted drawings, 119
    for photo-filled text, 137
    for sketched photo look, 121
flicker, 73
focal length of lenses, 30
focal planes in digital cameras, 29
Fog effect, 123, *123*
Folders tab, 140
fonts, 15
Foreground Color Frame option, 115
formatting memory cards, 33–34
frames
    color matching, **114–115**, *115*
    creating, **114**, *114*
    depth for, **116–117**, *116*
    scans for, **146–147**, *146–147*
    shape, **115–116**, *115–116*
    stylized strokes for, **158**, *158*
From Files and Folders option, 83
fully justified text, 23

G

gamma in calibration, 169–170
General Fixes palette, 97, *97*
Gothic typefaces, 16
gradients and Gradient tool
    for clip art, 141, **143**, *143*
    for text letters, **133**
graphics tablets, **70–72**, *70–72*
Graphire tablets, 71, *71*
grayscale, 12
GretagMacbeth tool, 168, *169*

H

hard drives
    for digital files, **76–77**, *77*
    for scanner images, **51**
hardware, **69**
    for archiving, **76–79**, *77–79*
    monitors, **72–74**

pen tablets, **70–72**, *70–72*
    for preserving images, **74–76**
harmony in color, 13
Horizontal Type Mask tool, 134
HP paper, 75
HP Photosmart 7960, 61, *61*
hue, 13
Hue/Saturation window, 104, *104*

I

ICC (International Color Consortium) standard, 168
image-editing software for scanners, **48–49**
image sensors
    in digital cameras, **29**
    in scanners, 42
image size and resolution, **100–101**
    in digital cameras, 31
    for frames, 146
    for pages, 154
ink-jet printers, **55–57**
    dpi and droplet size for, **57–58**
    ink colors and cartridges for, **58**, *58*
    ink types for, **59**, *59*
    maintaining, **62–65**
    maximum print size in, **59**
    preserving images from, 74
    selecting, **57**
    shopping lists for, **62**
    special features in, **59–61**
inks for prints, 75
Inner Shadows option, 116–117
interfaces
    in Photoshop Elements, 88
    for scanners, 46
International Color Consortium (ICC) standard, 168
interpolated pixels, 31
interpolated resolution, 44
Intuos tablets, 71
iPhoto, **86–87**, *87*

J

JPEG (.jpg) format, 76

L

lag, shutter-release, 32
laser printers, 57
Lasso tool, **102**, *102*
Layer visibility indicator, 93
layers and layer styles
    copying, **158–159**
    for effects, **111**, *111*
    for painting text, 132
    for text letters, **132–133**, *133*
    working with, 93
Layers palette, **92–93**, *92*
LCD screens
    batteries for, 34
    in digital cameras, 32, 37
LCDs (liquid crystal displays), 73
leading, 128
left aligned text, 21, *21*
lenses in digital cameras, **29–30**, 37
letter-sized backgrounds, **144–145**, *144–145*
letter-sized scanners for 12X12 pages, **160–165**, *161,*
    163–165
letters, text
    color for, 132
    filling, **132–133**
light in digital cameras, 29

lighting, 35
lightness, 12, 14
lines, drawing, **10**, *10*
lines of text, space between, 128
Linked layer indicator, 93
liquid crystal displays (LCDs), 73
Lock all option for layers, 93
Lock transparent pixels option, 93
logos, 24

M

macro settings in digital cameras, **34**
Magic Wand tool
    for clip art, 141
    for selections, **102**, *103*
Magnetic Lasso tool, 102
manual mode in digital cameras, 34
Marquee tool
    for backgrounds, 155–156
    for cropping, **107**, *108*
    for frames, 114
    for mosaic photo effect, 122
mass, **10–11**, *11*
mattes, **113–117**, *113–116*
maximum print size, 59
Maxtor hard drives, 76–77, *77*
MB (megabytes) in memory cards, 33
megapixels, 28
memory card slots, **60**
memory cards, **33–34**, *33*, 38
memory for scanner images, **51**
merging scanned images, **163–165**, *163–165*
Metadata tab, 140
Mona Lisa, 4, *4*
Monaco tool, 168
MonacoOPTIX tool, 168, *169*
monitors
    calibrating, 49, **72–74**, **168–170**, *169*
    shopping list for, **74**
    specifications for, **73–74**
monopods, 38
mosaic photo effect, **122–123**, *123*
Move tool
    for effects, 111
    for photographs, 158
    for sports trading cards, 125
movie mode, 36, *36*
multicard readers, **38–39**, *39*
multifunction printers, 43, *43*
museums, flash photography in, 33

N

negative space, rule of, **6**, *7*
negatives, scanning, **151–153**, *152*
New dialog box
    for punch shapes, 109
    for sports trading cards, 124, *124*
New Photomerge Panorama option, 163–164
Nickel Cadmium (NiCd) batteries, 34
Nickel Metal Hydride (NiMh) batteries, 34
Nikon Coolpix cameras, 28, *28*, 31, 35–36, *35–36*
Nikon D70 cameras, 28, *28*
noise levels in ink-jet printers, 59
nozzle checks for ink-jet printers, **64–65**, *65*

O

OCR (optical character recognition) software, 48
on/off buttons for ink-jet printers, **63–64**, *64*
one-button scanning, 46

opacity
    of background, 160, *160*
    of layers, 93
    for sketched photo look, 120
optical character recognition (OCR) software, 48
optical resolution of scanners, 44
optical viewfinders, 32
optical zoom, **30–31**, *30–31*
Optix colorimeter, 73
Organizer
    Auto Fix feature, 88, *88*
    for clip art, 140
    for contact sheets, 83
    workspace, **85–86**
organizing files, **85–87**, *86–87*
original images for scanning, 47

P

Page Setup dialog box, 153
Page Setup tab, 84
pages
    backgrounds for, **155–157**, *155–157*
    finishing, **160**
    page rules, **1**
        Rule of Balance, **2–3**, *2–3*
        Rule of Negative Space, **6**, *7*
        Rule of Thirds, **5–6**, *5–6*
        Rule of Visual Center, **3–4**, *4*
    parts gathering for, **154**, *155*
    photo placement on, **157–159**, *157–159*
    printing, **165–166**
    type for, **159**, *159*
Paint Bucket tool
    for frames, 116
    for punch shapes, 109
    for sketched photo look, 120
    for sports trading cards, 124
painted drawings from photographs, **117–119**, *117–119*
painterly finished images, **119–121**, *120–121*
painting text, **131–133**, *132–133*
Palette Bin, 92
palettes, **88–93**
paper
    for ink-jet printers, 60, 65
    for prints, 75
paper paths, 61
paragraphs, type for, 16
Paste Layer Style option, 159
patterns
    for clip art, **141–142**, *142*
    for text letters, **132–133**
PCMCIA slots, 39
pen tablets, **70–72**, *70–72*
Photo Compare, 86, *86*
Photo option for scanning, 47
photo printers, 43
Photo Review, 86
photo services, **65–66**, *66*
photographs
    black-and-white
        from color, **98–99**, *98–99*
        colorizing, **121–122**, *122*
    painted drawings from, **117–119**, *117–119*
    placement of, **157–159**, *157–159*
    printing, **153–154**
    scanning, **150–151**, *150*
    text in, **130–131**, *130–131*
    in text, **134–137**, *134–137*
Photomerge dialog box, 163, *163*
Photoshop Elements, **48–49**, 81
    backups for, **82–85**

benefits of, **82**
editing tools and palettes in, **88–93**
organizing files in, **85–87**, *86–87*
photosites in digital cameras, 29
PhotoSpin.com clip art, 140
picoliters, 57–58
pigments for prints, 75
pixel pitch, 73
pixels
in digital cameras, **28**
in monitors, 73
pixels per inch (ppi) for scanners, 48
PIXMA printers, 61, *61*
planning scans, **49–50**, *50*
Polygonal Lasso tool, 102
positioning
in pen tablets, **70–71**, *71*
photographs, **157–159**, *157–159*
PostScript, 61
ppi (pixels per inch) for scanners, 48
pressure-sensitive stylus control, 71
Preview tab, 140, *140*
primary colors, 13
Principle of Alignment, **21–23**, *21–23*
Principle of Contrast, **23–25**, *25*
Principle of Proximity, **20**, *20*
Principle of Repetition, **24**, *24*
print head alignment, 62
Print Photos dialog box, 84, *85*
Print Preview dialog box, 153, *153*, 165, *166*
printers
ink-jet. *See* ink-jet printers
multifunction, 43, *43*
types of, **56–57**, *56*
printing
pages, **165–166**
photo services, **65–66**, *66*
photographs, **153–154**
preserving images, **74–76**
print size and speed in, 59
profiling software, 72, **168–170**
Proximity Match for Spot Healing Brush, 104
punch shapes, **109–111**, *109–111*

Q

quality in digital cameras, 31
Quick Fix mode
for cropping, 99, *99*
working with, **88–89**, *89*, **96**
Quickly Fix Photos option, 87

R

radial balance, 2–3, *3*
Radius setting for sharpening, 105–106
RAM (random access memory)
for digital cameras, 33
for scanner images, **51**
ransom note style, 17, *17*
raster images, 131–132
RAW format, 76
rechargeable batteries, 34
Rectangular Marquee tool
for backgrounds, 155–156
for cropping, 107
for frames, 114
for mosaic photo effect, 122
red-eye correction, **96–97**, *96–97*
Red-Eye Removal tool, 96
reflective pieces in scanners, 42
refresh rate, 73

Remove Color option, 118
repetition, **24**, *24*
repetitive patterns for clip art, **141–142**, *142*
resampling, 100
resizing photos, 158
resolution
for clip art, 140
in digital cameras, **31–32**
and image Size, **100–101**
in monitors, 73
for pages, 154
for scanning, **44**, 47–48, 161
backgrounds, 144
photos, 150
slides and negatives, 152
restoration technology and software for scanning, **48**
retouching, **101–106**, *102–106*
Revert to Saved option, 90
RGB color, 121, 131
right aligned text, 21, *21*
RIP, 61
roll paper, 60
Roman typefaces, 16
round forms, 10
Rule of Balance, **2–3**, *2–3*
Rule of Negative Space, **6**, 7
Rule of Thirds, **5–6**, *5–6*
Rule of Visual Center, **3–4**, *4*

S

sans serif typefaces, **16**, *16*
saturation, color, 14, *14*
scanner beds, 44
scanners, 41
bit-depth of, **43**, *44*
computer connections to, **45–48**, *45*, *47*
DMax, 44
drivers for, 46
features of, **42–43**, *42–43*
image file size, 51
maintaining, **52–53**, *52–53*
merging images from, **163–165**, *163–165*
planning scans for, **49–50**, *50*
resolution of, **44**, 47–48, 161
for backgrounds, 144
for photos, 150
for slides and negatives, 152
settings for, **46–48**
shopping list for, 45
software for, **48–49**
scanning
12X12 pages, **160–165**, *161*, *163–165*
backgrounds, **144–147**, *144–147*
photographs, **150–151**, *150*
slides and negatives, **151–153**, *152*
scene settings in digital cameras, 35
screens in digital cameras, 32
script typefaces, **16**, *16*
SCSI cables, 45, *45*
secondary colors, 13
Selection Brush tool, **103**, *103*
selections, **101–102**
Lasso, **102**, *102*
Magic Wand, **102**, *103*
Selection Brush, **103**, *103*
sepia tone photos from color, **98–99**, *98–99*
serif typefaces, **16**, *16*
shade, 14
shapes, **10**, *10*, **109–111**, *109–111*
sharp corners, 10
Sharpen palette, 98

sharpening, **105–106**, *105–106*
shutter-release buttons, **32**
silver halide, 56, 74
Simple Sharp Pillow Emboss option, 146
single lens reflex cameras, 28, *28*
size
    contact sheets, 85
    image sensors, 29
    ink-jet printer droplets, 57–58
    ink-jet printers, 60
    photos, 158
    in scanning, 47
sketched photo look, **119–121**, *120–121*
slides, scanning, **151–153**, *152*
software, **69**
solid ink printers, 57
source images for scanning, 47
space between lines, 128
special effects. *See* effects
sports trading cards, **124–125**, *124–125*
Spot Healing Brush tool, 104, *105*
Standard Edit mode, 89, *89*
    cropping in, **106–107**
    palettes in, **92**, *92*
    retouching in, **101–106**, *102–106*
Stroke dialog box
    for frames, 158–159, *158*
    for text letters, 133
strokes for frames, **158–159**, *158*
Style Settings dialog box
    for frames, 147
    for text letters, 133
Styles and Effects palette
    for backgrounds, 156–157
    for clip art, 143
    for frames and borders, 114–117, *114*, 146, 158
    for mosaic photo effect, 123
    for photo-filled text, 136–137
    for text, 129, 133
    for type, 159
stylized strokes for frames, **158**, *158*
stylizing editable text, **128–130**, *128–130*
stylus pens, 70–72
surge protectors, 79
symmetrical balance, 2, *2*

T

tablets, **70–72**, *70–72*
tactile texture, 11–12
target images and sizes in scanning, 47, 50
teeth, whitening, **104**, *104*
telephoto lenses, 30
tertiary colors, 13
text
    alignment, **21–23**, *21*
    backgrounds and photos in, **134–137**, *134–137*
    effects, **127**
    painting, **131–133**, *132–133*
    in photographs, **130–131**, *130–131*
    scanning, 48
    stylizing, **128–130**, *128–130*
    warping, **129**, *129*
texture
    for clip art, **142–143**, *143*
    in pages, **11–12**, *12*
thermal wax printers, 57
thirds, rule of, **5–6**, *5–6*
Threshold setting for sharpening, 106
throwing up in color, 15
TIFF (.tif) format, 76

Tile Windows option
    for frames, 146
    for photographs, 157
tint, 14
titles, type for, 16
tonal range of scanners, 43
toolbar, **90–92**, *90–92*
Torn Edge effect, 156–157, *157*
trading cards, **124–125**, *124–125*
transitional colors, 13
transparency adapters, 42
Transparency option, 47
tripods, 38
TWAIN technology, 46
12X12 pages
    letter-sized scanners for, **160–165**, *161, 163–165*
    scanned backgrounds for, **145**, *145*
type, **15–17**, *17*
    for pages, **159**, *159*
    texture for, 11
Type layer indicator, 93
Type tools, 128–130, *128*
typefaces, **15–16**

U

Underpainting dialog box, 118, *118*
underwater housing for digital cameras, 35, *35*
uninterruptible powers (UPSs)
    for digital files, 77
    with ink-jet printers, 63
    purpose of, **79**, *79*
Unsharp Mask, 105, *106*
USB cables, 45, *45*
USB flash drives, **76**

V

value, **12**, *12*
Vertical Type Mask tool, 134
video cards, 74
viewable image size, 73
viewfinders, **32**
visual center, rule of, **3–4**, *4*
visual spectrum, 13
visual texture, 11–12
volume, **10–11**, *11*

W

Wacom tablets, 70–72, *71*
warm hues, 13
warping text, **129**, *129*
white balance, **34–35**
white points, 169–170
white space, **6**, *7*
whitening teeth, **104**, *104*
wide angle lenses, 30
Wind style, 156
workspaces
    Editor, **87**, *87*
    Organizer, **85–86**

Z

ZigZag dialog box, 157
zoom in digital cameras, **30–31**, *30–31*
Zoom tool
    for colorizing black-and-white photos, 122
    for red-eye correction, 96

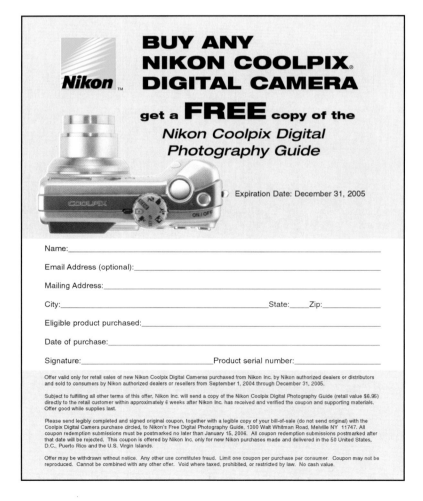

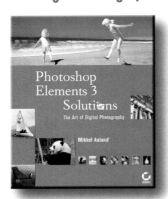

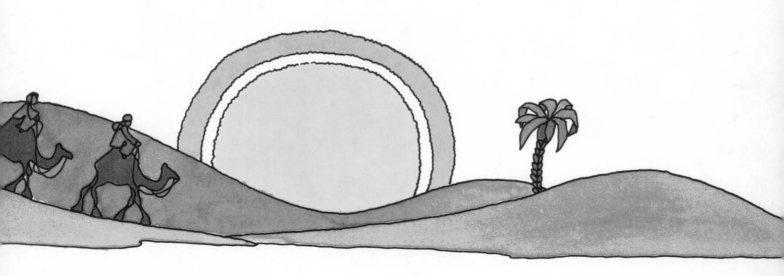

TEN BROTHERS
WITH CAMELS

by Gladys Y. Cretan

pictures by Piero Ventura

gb GOLDEN PRESS • NEW YORK

WESTERN PUBLISHING COMPANY, INC.

RACINE, WISCONSIN

Library of Congress Catalog Card Number: 73-84543

Golden, A Golden Book®, and Golden Press® are trademarks
of Western Publishing Company, Inc.

Today smells of spices
And roasting of meat.
A treat.
For today my uncles come for a feast.
They come from Marash and Haleb and Beirut,
And they each bring a camel to sell in the East.

They bring their camels this time every year.
Here,
I'll sit on this hill and watch them arrive.

My father belongs to a family of ten.
At first they were ten boys,
But now they're ten men.
Ten boys.
We'll count.

My uncles will come and they'll each bring a camel,
A splendid amount
When all put together in one caravan.
Enough for a sheik.
Or a Sultan.
Enough for me.

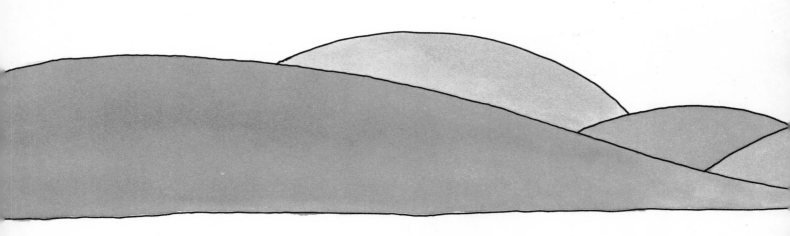

First is Uncle Kosrove, my father's oldest brother.
He comes with his camel.
And he is One brother
Who is here for the feast.

Next comes Levon, my father's quiet brother.
He doesn't say a word.
But when he sees me he nods.
And I know he's glad, not sad.

Now
There's Kosrove the oldest. He's number One.
And Levon who's quiet. He makes Two.
That's Two brothers, with camels,
Who've come for the feast.

The third one is Manoog,
With a voice that's uproarious.
His look is quite fierce,
His huge mustache is glorious.

Let's see,
That's Three brothers with camels
Who've come for the feast.

Look!
A double row comes over the hill.
That would be Miran and Diran. The twins.
They look alike.
They act alike.
We tell them apart by their hats.

So now....
There's Kosrove the oldest. He's number One.
And Levon who's quiet. He makes Two.
There's Manoog who's fierce. Manoog is Three.
And Miran and Diran are Four and Five.
Five brothers, with camels,
Who've come for the feast.

There's a whirling in the air,
And I know it's a juggler.
Uncle Sarkis is the juggler.
He juggles while he rides his camel.
He makes those balls spin, twirl, whoosh, whirl,
But never fall.
Sarkis the juggler is number Six.

Six brothers with camels,
Who've come for the feast.

Listen! Don't look.
You can tell from the sound
That Bedros is coming,
Our singer of songs.
His song gets here first, over the mound.
Then another sound...
His camel comes, his legs plod the ground.
They pound.
They pound.

Now count again.
There's Kosrove the oldest. He's number One.
And Levon who's quiet. He makes Two.
There's Manoog who's fierce. Manoog is Three.
And Miran and Diran are Four and Five.
Sarkis the juggler is number Six.
And Bedros the singer,
The singer makes Seven.
Seven brothers, with camels,
Who've come for the feast.

The next one is Aram, whose long beard is black.
The sack at his side carries almonds,
For selling,
For trading,
For me.
He, black-bearded Aram, is number Eight.

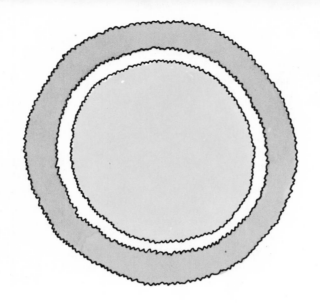

Eight brothers, with camels,
Who've come for the feast.

Last in the line comes Nazaret.
He's the biggest and strongest,
And wrestles the best,
Yet he's younger than all the rest.

Now let's count.
There's Kosrove the oldest. He's number One.
And Levon who's quiet. He makes Two.
There's Manoog who's fierce. Manoog is Three.
Miran and Diran are Four and Five.
Sarkis the juggler is number Six.
There's Bedros the singer.
The singer makes Seven.
Black-bearded Aram is number Eight.
And Nine in the line is young Nazaret.

But one must be missing, there are Ten in the set.
Nine brothers with camels to sell in the East.
And the Tenth?
Why it's Father!
Preparing the feast!

And while he prepares it, I have a job too.
I take each camel, and as fast as I can
I hook them together into one caravan.
And this time we know whom we mustn't leave out.
The camel of Father.

We'll count them again so there won't be a doubt.
One. Two. Three. Four.
Five. Six. Seven. Eight. Nine.
And what is one more?
Ten!

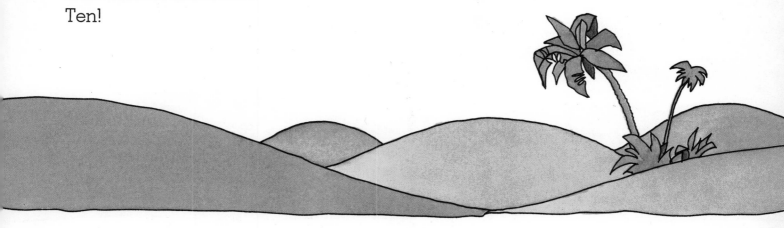

Here are ten camels, all in a line.
They're tied, and they're counted,

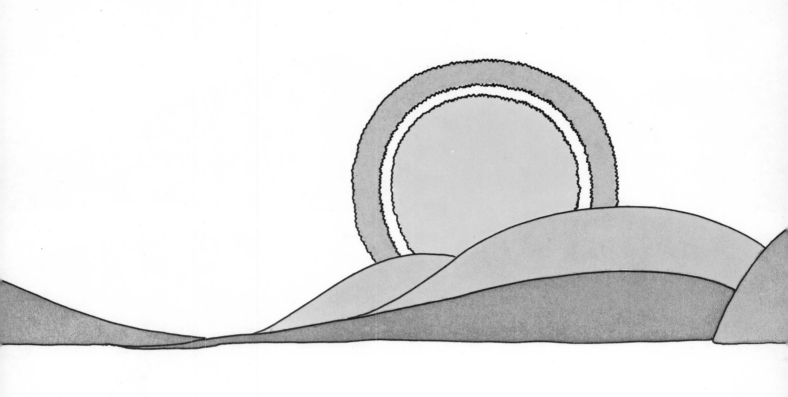

And after the feast
Ten brothers will lead them off to the East.